The Martyrs

A STUDY IN SOCIAL CONTROL

THE UNIVERSITY OF CHICAGO PRESS
CHICAGO, ILLINOIS

—

THE BAKER & TAYLOR COMPANY
NEW YORK

THE CAMBRIDGE UNIVERSITY PRESS
LONDON

THE MARUZEN-KABUSHIKI-KAISHA
TOKYO, OSAKA, KYOTO, FUKUOKA, SENDAI

The Martyrs

A STUDY IN SOCIAL CONTROL

By

DONALD W. RIDDLE

The University of Chicago

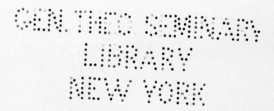
THE UNIVERSITY OF CHICAGO PRESS
CHICAGO · ILLINOIS

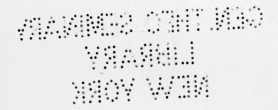

To
RUTH EMERY RIDDLE

PREFACE

It is hoped that this study of the early Christian martyrs may be useful for at least two purposes which are of contemporary interest. It is a notable feature of the modern study of religion that its psychological basis is familiarly known and that practical use of this knowledge is being made in social applications. Religion is increasingly regarded as one of the forces of social control. It is therefore desirable to study any set of phenomena which may throw light upon the processes, techniques, and methods of religion as such a force. Obviously the experiences of the martyrs furnish relevant data for such a study. These findings may be useful not only as an exhibit of religion as an agency in social control but as practical data for those who propose to utilize religion as a social force in modern situations.

The present study is, therefore, new. To be sure, the martyrs and the persecutions have been voluminously studied. However, it was other motives which have prompted the immense literature about them. A dispassionate approach, without theological bias or apologetic interest, which regards the persecutions of the Christians as group conflicts and which sees the deeds of the persecuted as the results of attitudes socially produced, is not only new but timely.

Second, the recent years have brought to articulation new methods in the study of early Christian literature. The German method of *Formgeschichte* and a historical method which is properly ascribed to Professor Shirley Jackson Case, of the University of Chicago, were contemporary in their appearance. The present study owes much to both these approaches, particularly to the latter. It is projected as a full and detailed application of social-historical method to one set of data. It is true, since the sources upon which it is based are inclusive both of the New Testament and certain extra-canonical writings, that in it the line between the New Testament and church-history disciplines is practically obliterated. Yet the study is based upon the conviction that the proper starting-point for many New Testament projects should be, as in this case, in the abundant sources of the second and the third centuries. Once the generalizations are worked out where the sources are adequate, the point of view there developed may be carried back to the periods in which the sources are meager.

It is on this plan that an analysis of the behavior of the martyrs becomes an application of social history to the study of the New Testament. It is by deliberate design that the method culminates in a study of certain of the traditional sayings of Jesus. Only by so adequate a perspective can a worthwhile result in the application of form or social history be achieved.

It hardly requires mention that the findings herein set forth are regarded as data for the technical use of sociologists. The author's training in the social sciences is secondary to his experience with the New Testament and early Christian literature.

The author wishes to acknowledge his obligation to Professor Shirley Jackson Case, of the University of Chicago. To Professor Edgar J. Goodspeed, of the University of Chicago, the author's debt, already great, is increased by reason of valuable advice and encouragement. This opportunity is embraced also to thank Mr. Donald P. Bean, of the University of Chicago Press, for kind assistance.

DONALD W. RIDDLE

THE UNIVERSITY OF CHICAGO
January 26, 1931

TABLE OF CONTENTS

I

PERSECUTION AND SOCIAL CONTROL

Although the Christian martyrs have been studied on the basis of several interests, their behavior as the result of social control has not heretofore been analyzed. Since the documents recounting their experiences happen to be among the sources for the study of the persecutions, the church historians have given them attention. Because their fate involved important points of Roman law, they have been of interest to jurists. The type of writing in which their stories were couched has led to research in the field of patristic literature. It goes without saying that the most obvious interest in the martyrs has been on the part of the hagiographers; the saints have been an important element in church lore, with the result that the tales told about them have multiplied and have been carefully compiled.

But the aspect of the behavior of the martyrs as the result of social control has not yet received adequate attention, though it is of the highest significance. It is obvious that control is a major factor of religion, and the experiences of the martyrs constitute an example of control which is most instructive. Clearly the fate which was suffered by not a few of them was one against which ordinary impulses vehemently rebel. Nevertheless, for certain reasons, and in spite of the usually held points of view, it was not unwillingly accepted. The willingness to undergo suffering is a social attitude which was present as the result of control. It follows that the behavior of the martyrs offers a field for investigation in which much may be learned of the technique of control as it is applied in the religious life, and the sources reflecting their experiences become a veritable laboratory of research.

For the martyrs, as the unfortunate victims of persecution, were involved in a situation in which one of the essential elements was the task of control. Indeed, it may be stated that any situation of persecution involves as its two primary aspects conflict and control. The persecuting group attempts to enforce its demands upon the persecuted; while the persecuted, unless, as sometimes happens, they submit to the demands of the persecutors, are under the necessity of controlling those of their number who are faced with the personal decision of the matters at issue. The persecutors attempt to control the persecuted, while the persecuted must control those who are or may become the victims of untoward activity.

The particular examples afforded by the Christian martyrs instructively illustrate these phenomena. In several cases the Roman state undertook to enforce conformity in religion upon its subjects; but many resisted its demands, apparently for reasons which at least were sufficient to themselves. As a matter of fact, they chose to conform to another religious pattern, and their maintenance of their choice meant simply the devotion to a counter loyalty. The group to which they preferred to be loyal had a sufficiently powerful influence upon them, and the values which from their point of view depended upon their fellowship were alluring enough that many persisted in their choice and were successful in their resistance of the state's demands.

Indeed, the elements of the situations which obtained in the best-known cases of Christian martyrdom were simple. The demand on the part of the state in the persecution of Decius, for example, made any subject liable to examination in court. Upon presenting himself, he was faced by a simple alternative: he might confess that he was a Christian, and be remanded for further discipline; or he might deny that he was a Christian, and, upon offering evidence to substantiate his denial, be set at liberty. This procedure reduced the situation to the barest simplicity for both the persecuting and the persecuted groups.

To take another example, the well-known letter of Pliny to Trajan reveals the same dichotomy. The governor's custom, he stated, was to ask the suspect during his examination whether he was a Christian. If he denied, he was immediately set free. If he admitted the fact, he was asked again and yet again; and, to induce the perception that it would be advisable for him to reply negatively, the question as reiterated was accompanied by threats. The alternative must have been altogether clear to the persons under trial.

Nothing can be more obvious than that the essential elements in such a situation were conflict and control. The state was attempting to enforce conformity to a pattern which it approved, while the Christian was faced with the necessity of affirming the loyalty desired by the state or persisting in his loyalty to the group which the state (and presumably the public in the majority) disapproved. On the part of the Christian group it is easy to see, as doubtless it was obvious to Christian leaders, that the crux of the matter was the necessity of controlling any suspected adherents so that they would maintain their loyalty to their own pattern, even though it was disapproved by the state.

So clear was this issue that it was recognized in its simplicity at an early date. When, in the early second century, the leaders of the Christian movement began to produce a literature of defense against the unfriendly attitude of the state, it was a point to which they directed vigorous protest that the crime of being a Christian was the sole offense upon the Roman legal calendar whose punishment might be evaded by merely denying guilt.[1] It is probable, also, that in few, if any other, cases was there so plainly indicated the desire of the state for the accused to avail himself of the privilege of acquittal by the easy means of denying his guilt. But this attitude on the part of the state officials is readily

---

[1] Justin *Apology I*, 4; Tertullian *Apology II*.

recognizable in not a few cases of anti-Christian action.[1]

Consequently, at an early stage in the relations between the Roman state and the Christian churches there developed a status which was purely dichotomous. In situations of widespread persecution, or in local situations where one person or a small group was subjected to coercion, the task of the group to which the victims belonged was clearly recognized. So fully was it perceived, indeed, that the terminology which was used to meet it became quite technical. In brief, the task of the Christian group was to secure from those of its adherents who were being tried a confession; while, on the other hand, it was the object of the state to induce them to deny the accusation that they were Christians. It is highly significant that the Christians took over the purely legal verbiage of the Roman court and made it a part of the religious vocabulary which had special meaning for them. Such usage of the terms "I confess" (Greek, ὁμολογέω) and "I deny" (Greek, ἀπαρνέομαι) is to be found in numerous specimens of the literature on persecution.

To say that the task of the Christian groups was clearly recognized is not to say that it was easy of performance. The disapproved group was aware that it must secure a confession and prevent a denial. But how were these objects to be attained? The apparent advantages were on the side of the state. Powerful forces operated in favor of doing what the

[1] Cf., for example, Tertullian *To Scapula; The Acts of the Scillitan Martyrs.*

imperial edict demanded. In the first place, to acquiesce in the royal order resulted in liberty and freedom from punishment; and, as the experiences of martyrdom and persecution multiplied, the punishments to which confessors were liable were of sufficient unpleasantness to warrant careful avoidance. But sanctions which were more subtle may have been equally effective. The status of respectability is usually highly desired; and in the case of the coercion of Christians by imperial Rome respectability, from the point of view of the majority, was on the side of the state. On the whole, it is usually easier to side with the majority in matters involving approval and disapproval; and, as is well known, behavior always involves these sanctions.

To be sure, not infrequently in minority groups social approval does not necessarily mean the taking-over of the patterns popularized by the majority. If such a group can convince its adherents that its own manner is better, it may secure conformity to the pattern of limited currency. But even though the Christian groups which were subject to persecution succeeded in impressing their suspected adherents that it was better to do as the few thought best than to do that which was demanded by the many, persecution presented the problem of confirming such an evaluation as threats, scorn, and force functioned to disturb the previously formulated judgment.

Yet the church vanquished the state in the issue of persecution. There were martyrs and confessors in sufficient number that the persecutions and the far more numerous local suppressions failed permanently to stem the tide of the new religion's popularity. The result makes obvious the fact that the Christian groups succeeded in their task, difficult as it was.

What is instructive in the process is the development, on the part of the churches, of techniques and methods of control. It hardly needs to be pointed out that the test of any religious movement is its ability to control its members to the point where their behavior exhibits the effect of the movement in shaping standards and patterns of conduct. Any such movement which possesses individuality has its particular standards and patterns; unless it ceases to exist, it must be able to make them effective in the behavior of those who belong to it.

In the case of early Christianity, its success, gauged by this criterion, was remarkable. Beginning as a group so obscure that it was not distinguished from Judaism, and in its beginning with a closely prescribed numerical and geographical distribution, it early gained wide expansion and successfully took its place beside other cults in the Empire. In the space of less than four centuries its growth was sufficient to enable it to absorb or supplant all other similar cults, until it became the only legalized religion of the Empire. During this time its increase in numbers witnessed its importance; Constantine's edict of toleration exhibits an unqualified recognition that Christians by that date formed an important element in the population. It goes without saying that, whether by its own contribution or by adaptation of current manners, Christianity stamped a well-defined pattern of religious type upon the Roman Empire.

To be sure, it is not suggested that the success of Christianity in establishing itself marked it as essentially different from contemporary religions. Research has shown that the contrary is true. Christianity succeeded because it took over a sufficient proportion of the religious interests common in its day that it to such an extent absorbed common interests and the public among whom they were current. But this is a matter outside the scope of the present study. All that is essential for the purpose at hand is the notation that the success of Christianity, which was remarkable, obtained because the movement, on the whole, became popular.

Such unpopularity as was coincident with the phenomena of persecution is likewise to be understood on social grounds. Christianity suffered the disability which in the Roman religious synthesis was inherent in newness; the Roman law explicitly designated any new cult as illegal. In that remarkable whole which was the religion of the Roman Empire, each new and foreign element, with the exception of the Cybele cult, was illegal until its popularity forced its general acceptance. Christianity was not the only religion to be suppressed by Roman law; the vicissitudes of the cult of Isis in Rome offer another example. The legal basis for the persecution of the Christians was perfectly sound.[1]

In addition to its illegality as a new cult, the Christian movement suffered other disabilities in the estimation of the general public. The general omission of the use of images was a feature in which Christians, like Jews, were regarded as peculiar. They, also like Jews, were popularly thought for this reason to be atheists.

In their common worship the behavior of Christians was highly emotional, and this fact led to other serious charges against them. Whatever may or may not have been the justice of the charge, there was a widespread belief that they practiced sexual immorality; and in the most extreme form of propaganda urged against them it was said that they were guilty of incest and of a form of cannibalism which involved the murder of children as victims.

Furthermore, Christians were popularly regarded as unpatriotic, since many of them absented themselves from public games and spectacles which were at once of a religious and a patriotic nature. Many omitted the observance of honors commonly paid to emperors on their birthdays. Some, at least, objected to, and advised others to evade, military service.

Still other matters urged against Christians are less explicit, but doubtless they operated to some degree in building up the attitudes of disfavor

[1] Canfield, *The Early Persecutions of the Christians* (New York, 1913).

against them which obtained in situations of persecution. Certain criticisms of the common way of life which were made by their more rigorous leaders rendered the ascetic Christians unpopular as fanatics always are. To the degree to which the fulminations of the apologists reflect the popular polemic against idolatry it is easy to see how the Christian, like the Jewish, conceptions of God and how he should be worshiped would react to the disfavor of those expressing them.

At all events, the popularity which accounts for the rapid spread of Christianity through the Empire was upon occasion countered by disfavor, which expressed itself in mob actions, local suppressions, and persecution properly so called. Whether the particular motive for anti-Christian action was a basic conservatism, such as characterized the persecution of Decius, or whether it was the unrationalized odium which is apparent in the judgment of Pliny, there were several occasions when Christians found themselves at variance with a common judgment.

But it was by maintaining its standard, and bringing about the removal of the objective of persecution, that victory was won by the Christian groups. They held their own ground until such time as organized and articulate disapproval was less apparent. Ultimately they regained their status of sufficient popularity to resume their aggressive prosecution of their propaganda. Unfortunately, the process cost the lives of some of their adherents, but victory won even for these the status of martyr.

What were the occasions when the martyrs attained their crowns of glory? It is necessary in sketching the outlines of these events to draw the fundamental distinction between persecution, properly so called, and such local or temporary actions as do not fairly belong in the category of persecution. In the relations between Christians and the Roman state there were but few occasions which may properly be identified as persecutions. To be sure, Christian tradition speaks of ten persecutions; but this number is reached by defining the term less rigidly than the facts demand, and by including traditions of dubious attestation. When it is recognized that only Decius, Valerian, and Diocletian (with his associates) undertook action against the Christians with the avowed purpose of eradicating the Christian movement, and, further, that all other actions against Christians were either local, temporary, or were merely the behavior of mobs, the propriety of the distinction is apparent. Its importance for the propaganda of control also speaks for itself.

By such distinction it follows that the traditional "persecution of Nero" cannot properly be called such. Indeed, there are some scholars who have questioned that there was during Nero's reign any action against Christians.[1] But whether or no, the doubt of a Neronic persecution is justified; merely

[1] Cf. Arnold, *Die Neronische Christenverfolgung; eine kritische untersuchung zur geschichte der ältesten kirche* (Leipzig, 1888).

to take the text of Tacitus as it stands involves the recognition of the fact that there was no attempt by this emperor to eradicate the Christian movement, of which he was probably unconscious, and of the further fact that if Christians suffered during his régime they suffered, not as Christians, but as victims of a trumped-up charge which had nothing to do with their religion.

Again, rigid terminology forbids the denomination of the so-called persecution of Domitian as such. In this case the action unfriendly to Christians which is reflected in early Christian literature[1] doubtless took place,[2] but it had as its basis the zeal of the officials (or perhaps of the people) of a particular province, and was so localized that it came short of a persecution proper. In such a case it does not appear that there was any attempt to eradicate the movement; certain Christians became involved in conflict with the zeal for the cult of the Emperor which throughout the imperial period had been popular in the province of Asia.

Nor may one speak otherwise of the occasions which made martyrs during the reign of Trajan. Ignatius of Antioch exhibits the attitudes characteristic of the deliberate martyr; and if, as is highly probable, the so-called First Letter of Peter[3] came out of the situation which is also described in the

[1] See below, pp. 163–79.

[2] But cf. Merrill, *Essays in Early Christian History* (London, 1924), pp. 148–73.

[3] See below, pp. 156–63.

Pliny-Trajan correspondence,[1] there was all but explicit recognition that suffering for the name of Christian was to be expected in this time and place. However, Trajan's answer to Pliny's question indubitably proves that no universal or aggressive attempt against the Christian movement was contemplated. Only such cases as were brought to the attention of the state in a localized area brought danger to Christians.

However, Pliny's statement of his procedure when it became necessary to take action against a Christian is a most instructive piece of information. It clearly appears that in as early a situation as this the purely dichotomous relation was in effect: Pliny would release any suspect who denied his guilt, and, indeed, he offered repeated opportunity to any suspect to avail himself of this easy means of escaping punishment. Further, his remark that a genuine Christian could not be induced to revile Christ demonstrates that the issue of control was accepted, in some cases successfully, by the Christian group. The legal basis for action against Christians is evident from as early a date as the Pliny-Trajan correspondence.[2] It is only the limitation of the unfriendly relation to the jurisdiction of Pliny which renders it impossible to regard this action as a persecution.

The next two occasions of the like nature which are reflected in literature seem to have been merely local mob actions. One of these, in Smyrna, result-

[1] Pliny *Epistle* x. [2] Canfield, *op. cit.*

ed in the martyrdom of about a dozen Christians, chief of whom was Polycarp, the bishop of this region.[1] The date, 155, places the event in the time of Antoninus Pius. The most instructive feature which attends it is the emergence of a new type of writing, the martyrology; the source known as *The Martyrdom of Polycarp* is at once among the oldest and best examples of the type.

The other case[2] was that in which the Christian communities of Lyons and Vienne, in Gaul, were subjected to abuse. This, which occurred in the period of Marcus Aurelius, was unquestionably a mob action purely and simply. It would appear that a remarkable degree of dislike of the local Christians was engendered, for the ill treatment of suspects was ferocious and a travesty of legal procedure. It is these features of illegality which make it obvious that the martyrs of Lyone and Vienne were unfortunate victims of a temporary and a local disturbance.

Decrees against Christians are alleged in another story of martyrdom[3] which appeared at about the same time. The death of the apologist Justin and certain associates indicates that for a time at least Christians were in danger in Rome. However, there is no evidence that others than Justin and his fellows were punished at this time, and the trial of

[1] "The Martyrdom of Polycarp," in Lake, *The Apostolic Fathers*, pp. 309–45.

[2] Eusebius *Church History* v. 1. 7 ff.

[3] *The Acts of Justin and His Associates.*

these appears to have been conducted within the proprieties of the Roman legal system.

A group of martyrs suffered during the time of Commodus in Carthage.[1] In their case those features which have been described as usual are altogether apparent. Not only were those who were tried given assurance of release if they denied their guilt, but they were positively urged to avail themselves of the privilege. They were even offered a thirty-day reprieve, during which time it was hoped that they would embrace their opportunity to evade punishment. But, according to the story, these, too, exhibited the attitudes which had by this time become usual. They were eager for death, and forced their judge to make them martyrs.

According to strict definition, then, it appears that there was no persecution, properly so called, of the Christians during the first and the second centuries. While, during these years, there had been occasional and local outbreaks in which Christians suffered, there had been no attempt on the part of the state to proceed against the movement as such or to attempt to wipe it out completely. Save for these occasional and local difficulties, the Christian movement profited by the state's unconsciousness of it, and took the opportunity to grow and expand. Although the details of its early history are unfortunately obscure, it is safe to infer that its growth was, if not steady, at least sufficient to afford the basis for a development in the first half of the third

[1] *The Acts of the Scillitan Martyrs.*

century which enabled it to win the issue when its very existence was threatened by state opposition.

The period of the early third century was one of great importance for early Christianity. It had come to terms with the various social groups of the Empire, so that the process of assimilation which resulted in the remarkable synthesis which presently characterized the movement was achieved. Its character as an ecclesiastical movement was apparent; the local churches possessed a specifically organized officiary, practiced cult rites, and were characterized by a way of life which had sufficient distinction to mark it as Christian. It would appear from the events which soon occurred that their membership was inclusive of great numbers—so many, in fact, that the process of indoctrination could not keep pace with numerical growth. The fact that the movement was conscious of itself as one of the established religions of the Empire appears from its literature of defense.[1] That it was developing intellectual organization points also to its approach to the status of maturity.[2]

The state's consciousness of the importance of Christianity was expressed in the anti-Christian actions of Septimius Severus, Decius, and Valerian. The danger to members of the Christian churches in face of the action of Septimius Severus was mitigated only by the variation in the degree of severity

[1] Cf. Justin *Apology* I, II; Athenagoras *A Plea for the Christians;* Tertullian *Apology; To Scapula.*

[2] Cf. Origen *De Principiis.*

with which his edict was put into effect by his officers.[1] But there was little such mitigation in the case of the persecution of Decius. His determined effort was indeed a severe trial for the Christians. An avowed conservative, Decius made a comprehensive and a determined effort to uproot the Christian movement altogether, with a plan which was sufficiently broad in scope and detailed in specification to demonstrate the thoroughgoing character of his intention.

Apparently Decius planned the universal application of a test which was designed to determine the loyalty of his subjects to religious rites approved by the state. According to his edict,[2] all subjects were required to present themselves at appointed times and places and to perform such religious rites as were prescribed. Any persons who failed to meet this test were open to suspicion, and were specifically required to appear or be fetched. Refusal to meet the requirement was followed by imprisonment, with the further possibility of torture and death. As in other cases, the performance of the prescribed rites secured release from suspicion and from liability to punishment.

Obviously this was persecution properly so called. That the situation was vastly different from preceding unfriendly actions is evident from the result. Immediately upon the publication of the edict there were numerous defections from Christian adher-

[1] Tertullian *To Scapula* 4.

[2] Cf. Gregg, *The Decian Persecution* (Edinburgh, 1897), pp. 68 ff.

ence. Many Christians, even including certain
noted officials, hastened to observe the appointed
requirements, although, as they did so, the crowds
jeered. Others withdrew into a safe seclusion until
the edict might be withdrawn. Still others bribed
the officials whose duty it was to carry out the imperial decree, and thus were relieved of the necessity of appearing before the court. *Libelli*, or official statements that the requirement had been met,
were issued to certify a suspect's innocence; and
many of these, it would seem, were secured by
bribery.

But, on the other hand, confessors were also numerous, and martyrs not few. Apparently the
Christians as religious societies met the situation
with a method which was sufficiently effective to
hold their groups together until the persecution was
given over. The result was plain: Decius' persecution did not succeed in eradicating Christianity. To
be sure, it was not long continued, else the result
might have been different; but at all events it
failed of its objective.

A refinement in method is to be noted in the persecuting activity of Valerian.[1] Apparently the attempt made by Decius had demonstrated the im-
possibility of displacing an illegal religious movement by making its devotees liable to capital punishment. Perhaps it was the perception of this fact
which led Valerian to direct his activity against the
leaders of the churches. But even this narrowing of

[1] Eusebius, *Church History* vii. 11.

the issue was presently made more explicit. When it was first put into effect, the opportunity of recantation was offered the clergy, as in previous examples of anti-Christian action. But, without doubt to secure greater effectiveness, this privilege after a time was withdrawn, and an official of the Christian movement was liable to death if found guilty. However, a lay Christian might still secure release by recantation. With this severe restriction were others to the effect that assembly for public worship was forbidden, and the use of cemeteries for Christians was prohibited. As might be expected, so specific an attack was efficient; and only Valerian's death relieved a very difficult situation.

Unquestionably the severest persecution which the Christians were called upon to meet was that which occurred during the administration of Diocletian and his associates and which continued until Constantine's rise to power.[1] The Empire was by this time greatly altered by Diocletian's plan of fourfold administration, which was particularly unfortunate for the Christians, since his associates were even more opposed to Christianity than he was. An edict was issued which to the several clauses of Valerian's added the further points that church buildings were to be demolished, copies of Scriptures burned, church officials were to lose their civil rights, and laymen found guilty of being Christians were to be reduced to the rank of slaves. A further edict ordered the imprisonment of all

[1] Eusebius Church History viii. 4; Lactantius Of the Death of the Persecutors.

clergy; and when Diocletian was unable longer to restrain his associates, the most severe of all measures was adopted: the order was promulgated that being a Christian was a capital crime, and the test to determine guilt was required to be made universally.

It is also interesting that during this persecution a definite attempt was made to subvert the currency of Christianity by organizing propaganda of counter-teaching.

Indubitably, the last persecution was by far the most severe of all. Its effect was pronounced. Perhaps if persecution had been applied systematically in the West, where Christianity was weakest, rather than in the East where it was strongest, the result might have been different; but as a matter of fact, the most aggressive leadership, which meant the severest application of pressure, was in the East. As it was, the movement, through the opposition which it developed, survived even this terrible experience until the edict of Galerius relieved the situation and that of Constantine brought lasting peace.

It is therefore possible to generalize the main features of the situations of persecution. In the early days of Christianity's development the unfriendly reactions against the movement did not have uniform features, for which a definite technique might be worked out. Rather, the earlier suppressions which brought a response in Christian literature were unexpected and sudden. They took the Christian groups by surprise, and were regarded with dread and horror. But the persecutions proper, and those measures whose method more nearly approached the character of persecution, were carried on with relatively uniform features. The duality of the opposing systems was consciously felt by both parties, so that the attempt of the state might be met by corresponding effort on the part of the churches. The processes involved—for example, arrest, examination, threatening and persuasion, the offer of acquittal upon recantation, and the ultimate test of performing approved rites—might be matched by measures worked out by the leaders of the persecuted groups. The lack of generality of the anti-Christian attitudes, such as was evidenced by the lenience on the part of certain state officials in enforcing the requirements of several of the edicts, was an important lightening of the burden. But most important of all was the success of the persecuted groups in developing a technique of opposition, for it was this which won the victory for the church.

It is most significant that the cases of martyrdom which have figured in the literature reflect with the martyr the group of which he was one. By the time of the persecutions proper the Christian movement possessed a well-articulated organization which greatly assisted it in effecting sustaining power. In other words, Christian churches were already what may fairly be called "ecclesiastical groups." Thus, opposed to the other social entity, the state, there was another aggregate of social forces in conflict. The Christian group was in the conflict not hopelessly disadvantaged, for, as was pointed out, persecution was never universally and unremittingly applied. There was at least the possibility that loyalty to the group might be maintained if the technique to secure loyalty were known and applied.

It was a question of group loyalty, a question to which group the suspected Christian should manifest his loyalty. Should he align, or, as the case might be, realign his religious fellowship with groups approved by the state; or would the influence of his Christian fellowship be strong enough to induce him to entertain danger to maintain it? In Christianity from an early date social satisfactions were effected through group relations. While certain emphases—for example, the Pauline conception of redemption—were individualistic, the mode of their realization was social. Pliny called attention to the custom of the Christians to meet for common worship and a common meal. Later the highly ritualistic Eucharist possessed a powerful social effect. By the time of the persecutions the bond of common worship and ritual was strengthened as meetings were held in edifices owned by one of the group or, more particularly, by the group corporately. Were there any doubt of the consciousness of social solidarity on the part of the Christians, it could not survive the witness of non-Christian contemporaries to the fact.

It follows that when a suspected Christian was brought before a court and faced with the alternative of confessing or denying the guilt of being a Christian, his status at the moment was largely affected by the fact that he was one of a church group. To be sure, he was an individual (which can mean no more than that he was himself), but so to designate him does not wholly account for his status. The individuality which he possessed was his largely because he belonged to groups which influenced him, of which his Christian fellowship was one. He had associated with others who made up the total of his group relationships; he shared the standards of certain groups, and had learned with and from his fellows those attitudes which characterized him as a member of a religious society. He knew to some extent with what approval or disapproval his decision would be regarded by his fellows.

He was, to be sure, in a situation where habits, ordinarily considered, would not be adequate guides. It was a situation of unfamiliarity and uncertainty. Yet even in this situation there were certain elements developed by previous experience which might be useful to him. The essential matter was, from the point of view of the religious group of which he was one, to resolve the dubious elements in the situation so that his behavior might be made predictable. Such influences must be brought to bear as would secure the outcome desired by the group. The Christian who was being examined, or who might later be examined, must be controlled. Obviously, there was the possibility that under pressure he might adopt the attitude urged by the state, and renounce his present loyalty. Threats of punishment and death were powerful arguments. Such conflicting values furnished the problem.

The suspect might be influenced, on the one hand, by the immediate advantages to be gained by complying with the order of the state: acquittal, freedom, life. Or, he might keep before him as his sufficient motive the values to be gained by refusing to conform. As shall be shown, there were many who found the values of the Christian group sufficient to warrant persistent refusal to obey the state, and their example was powerful enough to carry many another confessor through the experience of martyrdom.

Now, the accused might conceivably resolve the dubious elements of the situation by deliberating over them. Even so, previous preparation was important. Whence came the values which were in his mind? Obviously he came to his present position with more or less equipment which had been obtained from previous experience. He had to a certain extent been indoctrinated, so that he held items of faith with more or less distinct imagery. He had shared group standards, and consequently these were to some degree influential.

As shall be shown, the Christian groups bent serious effort to assist in the resolution of the doubtful elements in the dilemmas before prospective martyrs. They undertook to prepare such persons as were likely to be examined, so that these would be ready to offer the answer desired by the religious fellowship, hoping thus to inhibit the tendency toward the opposite response. They exerted control even during the conduct of the examination; and after a confession had been made, they frequently found it possible and valuable to keep in touch with the martyr-designate.

The Christian groups accomplished their task by following a specific method. The process was essentially as follows: to secure from its adherents the behavior which was necessary if the movement were to survive, rewards of a sufficiently compelling nature were held forth, so that in the person being examined, or likely to be examined, there would be generated a wish to maintain his present relation. Negative sanction was secured by threatening punishment for failure to do so. The desired goal was repeatedly called to attention by careful visualization. Its realization by others was frequently pictured as a glorious fact. Encouragement was given by the thought of the participation of others in similar experiences, and it was pointed out that failure or success would be witnessed by one's fellows. In specific detail proper attitudes were suggested, stock answers to the prospective questions were taught, and stereotyped arguments were supplied, together with persuasive evaluations and heroic imagery. The attempt was made to induce in the candidate an emotion of overpowering character, so that he might be carried, if he had been sufficiently prepared, through the harrowing experience with a minimum of exception to the type of behavior which had been found to be desirable.

The facts demonstrate that the method followed by the Christian groups was successful to the point that not a few Christians accepted a fate against which the most basic impulses normally rebel. The values urged were sufficiently appealing that they, rather than those urged by the state, were chosen; and in many cases the choice was persisted in even in the face of harrowing torture. The churches secured enough confessions that the disintegration of the Christian movement was prevented. It is a witness to the skill of the churches, or of their leaders, that they utilized heroic experience to strengthen the resistance of others. It proved that the blood of the martyrs was the seed of the church.

II

THE PREPARATION OF THE MARTYR

It was the task of the Christian groups in situations of persecution to induce those of its adherents who were subject to examination to make a "confession," and to assist the confessor to maintain his resolution even though to do so meant torture or even death.

To be sure, there were occasions when early and sporadic actions against Christians precipitated occasions which had to be met without consciousness of this necessity or acquaintance with the technique by which such situations might be met. It appears that in several such cases there were martyrs whose experiences, and the attitudes which led to the experiences, arose, so to speak, spontaneously. The unnamed confessors who appear in the letter of Pliny were such. Perhaps Ignatius of Antioch is an example. The martyr Antipas of Pergamum, mentioned by name in the New Testament Apocalypse, certainly was one.

But what makes the experiences of the martyrs instructive is that when persecutions properly so called occurred, the Christian groups met them, and won the apparently unequal contest, by the preparation of the martyrs, so that confessions were secured and confessors confirmed in their resistance to the demands of the state.

The preparation of the martyrs was a process which ranged from extreme informality to specific organization. Of course in the earlier situations technique and method of control had not been acquired, so that it was only in the persecutions proper that the fully worked-out process of control may be seen in operation. The earlier periods are instructive for their evidence of the development of technique.

It was first necessary to induce in the prospective martyr a willingness to undertake the experience, even though he knew it to be unpleasant. The wish for the experience was reinforced by such sanctions as were found to be effective. Rewards for success were suggested with definite imagery, and punishments for failure were pictured with no less specificity. The effect of group contacts was utilized, and from such social influences proper attitudes were engendered and crystallized by powerful indoctrination. All such steps in the process may be seen in the sources which reflect situations of persecution.

Many known cases establish the fact that there were Christians who were not only willing to undergo the dangers of state examination but actually eager to do so. Ignatius of Antioch apprehended that his co-religionists in Rome might in some manner secure his release from such danger, and he wrote to them in all seriousness to refrain from making the attempt (*To the Romans* vii; v. 2. 6). He wished to die a martyr. In some cases Christians not only refused to avail themselves of the opportunity to escape but presented themselves for examination, while the officer in charge of the legal proceedings regarded their eagerness to die as hardly short of suicide (Tertullian *To Scapula* 5). Such cases demonstrate the presence in certain Christians of a wish to undertake the experience of confession. This wish was present in some, as shall be shown, by reason of a certain abnormality; but, as shall also be shown, in others it was present because it was generated by the action of the groups to which they belonged.

The sanction of reward for the successful survival of the experience of confession was perhaps the most elemental, and doubtless the most effective, of all the arguments which may be discovered in the preparation of the martyr. At any rate, it appears most voluminously in all the records in which the process is reflected. For example, it was frankly and explicitly urged by Tertullian, who upon one occasion wrote that "we are not in any great perturbation or alarm about the persecutions which we suffer, for we have attached ourselves to this sect fully accepting the terms of its covenant, so that, as men whose very lives are not our own we engage in these conflicts, our desire being to obtain God's promised rewards, and our dread lest the woes with which he threatens an unchristian life should overtake us" (*ibid.* 1). Another leader stated, "We are persuaded that when we are removed from the present life we shall live another life, better than the present one, and heavenly, not earthly . . . . or,

falling with the rest, a worse one and in fire"
(Athenagoras *A Plea for the Christians* 21). Even
an earlier perception of the issue popularizes the
balanced values in the form of a vision; picturing
the condition of the confessors, one asks what they
suffered, and was told "stripes, imprisonments,
great tribulations, crosses, wild beasts, for the
Name's sake. Therefore, to them belongs the right
side of the holiness of God, to them and to all that
suffer for the Name" (*Shepherd* of Hermas, *Vision*
3:2).

The rewards accruing from confession, and the
punishments which were the payment of denial,
were pictured with great definiteness, such definiteness, indeed, that candidates firmly believed that
confession was better than denial or than evasion
of the issue. So effectively was the point urged, and
so tenaciously was it believed, that reward was the
major sanction in preparing the martyr for confession.

It must be understood that not merely a hope of
reward was offered but that rewards were assured
with exact specification. What the rewards were
may readily be discovered. For one thing, it was
important to some of the early Christians that
death by martyrdom guaranteed resurrection from
among the dead, or, as the Greek rather than Jewish thought-patterns of life after death became current, the immediate and personal immortality of
the martyr. Tertullian characterized martyrdom as
"the true resurrection from God" (*Apology* 50) and

stated that the life-blood of the martyrs was "the sole key to paradise" (*On the Soul* 55). It was assured the readers of an early description of martyrdom that those who had confessed and died had by "a single hour's torture purchased everlasting life" (*Martyrdom of Polycarp* ii. 3), while of the most conspicuous hero of this occasion it was said that he was "crowned with the crown of immortality" (*ibid*. xvii. 1). The maintenance of confession was characterized as "the spoil of life eternal" (Tertullian *On the Resurrection of the Flesh* 43), and prospective martyrs were urged to "think less of death than of immortality" (Tertullian *Apology* 50).

The value of immortality was by some leaders urged with the greatest extravagance. For example, Cyprian, the bishop of Carthage, wrote, "Let no one think of death, but of immortality; not of temporary punishment, but of eternal glory. . . . . When you reflect that you shall reign and judge with Christ the Lord you must needs exult and tread under foot present sufferings, in the joy of what is to come" (*Epistle* lxxx. 2). What is perhaps the most extreme putting of the suggestion is by the same writer: "What more glorious, or what more blessed, can happen to any man . . . . than to confess the Lord God in death itself before his executioners? Than among the raging and varied and exquisite tortures of worldly powers, even when the body is racked and torn and cut to pieces, to confess Christ . . . . with a spirit still free, though departing? Than to have mounted to heaven with the world left behind? Than, all worldly impediments broken through, to stand already free in the sight of God? Than to enjoy the heavenly kingdom without delay? Than to have become an associate of Christ's passion in Christ's name?" (*ibid*. xxv).

Another value which it was alleged was guaranteed by martyrdom was the forgiveness of sins. Since sin is an ever present problem to the religious person and the religious group, it is no accident that the early Christians saw in martyrdom a means of securing the satisfactory solution of a troublesome question and used this as a sanction to induce the martyr attitude. As early a source as the *Shepherd* of Hermas states that the sins of all who have suffered for the Name have been taken away because they suffered for the Name of the Son of God (*Sim.* ix. 28. 3). As might be expected, the ardent Tertullian is eloquent at this point: "Who does not desire to suffer . . . . that he may from God obtain complete forgiveness, by giving in exchange his blood? For that secures the remission of all offences" (*Apology* 50). Again, he affirms, "There cannot any longer be reckoned aught against the martyrs, by whom in the baptism [of blood] life itself is laid down" (*Scorpiace* 6).

Tertullian, it is obvious, was an enthusiast; but even the intellectual Origen saw in martyrdom one of the seven means of obtaining the forgiveness of sins (*Homily on Leviticus* 24). Yet it must be conceded that the emotional Carthaginians reacted most violently to this value; it is in the pseudo-

Cyprianic *In Praise of Martyrdom* that the sanction is urged most extremely. In this work martyrdom is pictured as

expiating any kind of defilement of life, and the foulness of a polluted body, and the contagions gathered from the long putrefactions of vices and the worldly guilt incurred by so great a lapse of time, by the remedial agency of one stroke, whereby both reward may be increased and guilt excluded. Whence every perfection and condition of life is included in martyrdom [*ibid*. 2].

In the same source the height of hyperbole is reached: "O blessed ones! and such as truly have your sins remitted—if, however, you who are to be compared with Christ ever have sinned!" (*ibid*. 30).

The value of this sanction must be regarded in the perspective of the ancient world. Sin to the early Christians and their contemporaries was a very genuine problem, in which the concomitant notions of depravity, evil nature, and lost status of the natural man required a belief in something like a cosmic transformation. The practical equation of the redemptive value of martyrdom with the redemptive death of Christ is significant.

A still more vivid impression of the value of martyrdom was disseminated by the promises that it secured special place and privilege after its accomplishment. For instance, Cyprian wrote to a group of confessors,

Already breathing only celestial things, you ascend to loftier heights, even by the delay of your sufferings and by the long lapse of time you are not wasting, but increasing your glory. . . . . Your praises are as numerous as the days; as the months roll onward, ever your merits increase. He conquers once who suffers once, but he who continues always battling with punishments and is not overcome with suffering, is daily crowned [*Epistle* xv. 1].

Further, "The longer your strife, the loftier will be your crown" (*ibid*. xv. 3). In formal argument the bishop avers, "In proportion to the greatness of the injustice of our persecution, so will be the justice and the severity of the vengeance exacted for those persecutions" (*Treatise* v. 17).

The degree of reward corresponding to the severity of suffering is explicitly pictured. Of a group of imprisoned confessors, it is said that

part still abide in the dungeons of the prisons, or in the mines and in chains, exhibiting by the very delays of their punishments greater examples for the strengthening and arming of the brethren, advancing by the tediousness of their tortures to more ample titles of merit, to receive as many payments in heavenly rewards as days are now counted in their punishments [Cyprian *Epistle* lxxvi. 1].

Apparently—so full is the literature of such imagery—the desire to undergo martyrdom for the sake of reward was not uncommon. This was true even in cases where the grewsomeness of punishment was fully realized: "These things, though exceedingly painful, yet have been calmly endured by many, and have even been eagerly desired for the sake of fame and glory," Tertullian said (*To the Martyrs* 4). This attitude may explain the readiness with which certain martyrs were said to have "set before their eyes an escape from the fire which is everlasting and is never quenched, and with the eyes of their heart they looked up to the good things which are preserved for those who have endured" (*Martyrdom of Polycarp* ii. 3).

Doubtless such was the purpose of the exhortation to future martyrs to "let the offerings and the distinctions prepared come before you" (*In Praise of Martyrdom* 11). It is thus, at any rate, that Cyprian accounts for the martyrs' behavior: "They exult in the Lord, and rejoice and are glad in their God, and the adversities and evils of the world they bravely suffer, because they are looking forward to gifts and prosperities to come" (*Treatise* v. 20). The fact that Cyprian himself delayed his own martyrdom is explained by his biographer by recourse to this conception: "He might, indeed, have hastened to the crown of martyrdom appointed for him had it not been needful for him to have passed through all grades of glory, and thus to have arrived at the highest" (*Life and Passion of Cyprian* 7). Similarly, a later description of the martyrdom of Ignatius ingenuously states that the martyr "inwardly reflected that the confession which is made by martyrdom would bring him into a yet more intimate relation with the Lord" (*Martyrdom of Ignatius* 1).

How variously, as well as how richly, these values were urged is seen throughout the abundant literature. For example, Tertullian, with obvious reference to the figures of the New Testament Apocalypse, cites the tree of life, exemption from the second death, the hidden manna, the stone of glistening whiteness, the power to rule with a rod of iron, the brightness of the morning star, being clothed in white raiment, the name included in the book of life, being a pillar in the temple of God, and sitting with the Lord on his throne (*Scorpiace* 12). A group of confessors themselves wrote to their bishop Cyprian, to the effect that

we have received great joy, great comfort, great refreshment, especially in that you have described, with glorious and deserved praises, the glorious—I will not say deaths, but —immortalities of the martyrs . . . . with our eyes . . . . we have contemplated them seated among angels, and the powers and dominions of heaven. Moreover, we have . . . . perceived . . . . the Lord giving them the promised testimony in the presence of the Father. It is this, then, which also raises our spirits day by day, and inflames us to the following of the track of such dignity [Cyprian *Epistle* xxv. 2].

The ecstatic moment in which the Lord kisses the martyr is pictured,[1] as is the throneroom newly fitted up for each newcomer.[2] Such contemplation, Cyprian urged, should fill the confessor with joy:

What must be the vigor . . . . of your victorious consciousness, what the loftiness of your mind, what exultation of feeling, what triumph of your breast, that every one of you stands near to the promised reward of God, that you are secure from the judgment of God. You walk in the mines with a body captive, indeed, but with a heart reigning, you know that Christ is present with you, rejoicing in the endurance of his

---

[1] Cyprian *Epistle* lxxx. 4.   [2] Tertullian *On the Soul* 55.

servants, who are ascending by his footsteps and by his paths to the eternal kingdoms! You daily expect with joy the saving day of your departure, and, already about to withdraw from the world, you are hastening to the rewards of martyrdom, and to the divine homes, to behold after the darkness of this world the purest light, and to receive a glory greater than all the sufferings and conflicts [*Epistle* lxxvi. 7].

In this conception, as in others, the extremity of affirmation is found in the pseudo-Cyprianic *In Praise of Martyrdom:* "Inestimable is the glory of martyrdom, infinite its measure, immaculate its victory, immense its triumph, because he who is presented to him with the special glory of the confessor is adorned with the kindred blood of Christ" (*ibid.* 29).

Still other values were alleged to be secured by martyrdom. One of these, of much greater significance in the ancient world than in the modern scientific world-view, was the triumph over those demonic powers which were so real to the early Christians.[1] Another was the ability to intercede for one's earthly companions,[2] while others were the authority to judge one's judges[3] and the position of coregent with Christ.[4]

It is, of course, not to be supposed that the urging of these values was effective in all cases in control-

---

[1] Origen *Against Celsus* viii. 44.

[2] Cyprian *Treatise* iii. 17; Eusebius *Martyrs of Palestine* vii. 11.

[3] Tertullian *To the Martyrs* 2; Eusebius *Church History* vi. 42. 5; Origen *Exhortation to Martyrdom* 28; *Acts of the Scillitan Martyrs*.

[4] Rev. 20:4; *Acts of the Scillitan Martyrs*; Origen *Exhortation to Martyrdom* 28.

ling the behavior of those subject to coercion by the
state. Doubtless many, faced with the alternative,
preferred life and liberty to a glorious reward which
was obtained only through torture and death. The
abundant use of the sanction of reward does, however, indicate that, in the cases where control was
successful and confessions were secured and maintained, the willingness to undergo the unpleasant
experience was in large measure present because the
confessor was influenced by such promises as have
been illustrated. Many confidently believed that
the otherworldly rewards were worth more than
life on the condition laid down by the anti-Christian forces.

It is also clear that the willingness to undergo
punishment for the crime of being a Christian was
largely induced by the fear of the consequences of
failing to confess. The threat of punishment in the
afterworld was urged with co-operative force with
the rewards which were at the same time promised.
In this matter, again, the sanctions were various,
ranging from the exclusion from the religious group
to alleged fates of a cosmic consequence. The
thought that denial not only would entail the loss
of fellowship with the church group but would result in eternal punishment in the afterworld appears to have been of considerable influence in inducing the attitude of willingness to suffer as the
result of confession. At any rate, the literature of
martyrdom repeatedly suggests the fact.

Examples are plentiful. Only a representative few

need be cited. The so-called *Epistle to Diognetus* contrasts the apparent death of the world with the death which is real, and is kept for deniers, the everlasting fire which shall punish to the end. This, it states, will cause the fire of punishment to be regarded as a blessing (*ibid.* x. 7, 8). The story of Polycarp says that the martyrs of Smyrna "set before their eyes an escape from the fire which is everlasting and is never quenched" (*Martyrdom of Polycarp* ii. 3). Athenagoras contrasts the blessed state of the martyrs with the fate of the deniers who suffer in fire (*A Plea for the Christians* 21). Cyprian marvels that deniers do not fear God, who threatens eternal punishment to those who deny him (*Epistle* lxxvi. 5), and exhorts some fellow-clergymen that they shall have before their eyes the fear of God and of eternal sufferings rather than the fear of men and of temporary discomfort (*ibid.* ii). Those who obey the devil and sacrifice to idols, he affirmed, will suffer the torments threatened by the Lord at judgment (*ibid.* lxiii. 2).

In this matter, as in others, it is the rhetorical pseudo-Cyprian who is most graphic. His *Praise of Martyrdom* insists that the punishment of denial is as certain as is the reward of confession (*ibid.* 19, 11). In the same work the punishments are pictured very definitely:

A horrible place, of which the name is Gehenna, with an awful murmur of souls bewailing, and with the flames belching forth through the darkness of thick night. There are many degrees of its violence . . . . it punishes with different dooms. Some are bowed down with an intolerable load, some are hurried by a merciless force over the abrupt descent of a precipitous path, and the heavy weight of clanking chains bends over them in bondage. Some a wheel is turning and an unwearied dizziness is tormenting, so that both fire is devouring and the load of iron is weighing down, and the uproar of many is torturing [*ibid*. 19, 20].

But it was not by threats of future punishment merely that control was effected. Specific misfortunes immediately following denial were alleged. Cyprian, for example, related a series of such (*Treatise* iii. 24–26). One denier was forthwith stricken dumb. Another was seized by an evil spirit and made to bite out her own tongue, death quickly following. A little child who was fed with the sacrificial food quickly became dumb, with symptoms of hysteria following, and, later, when the Eucharist was offered it, the elements could not be retained. A certain woman who denied was seized by a frenzy. When another denier attempted to resume his fellowship in his church, he found that the eucharistic bread turned to a cinder in his hand. Great numbers of deniers were alleged to have become possessed by evil spirits, fallen into idiocy and insanity, while many suffered death. It is hardly necessary to remark that these stories are to be taken seriously only to the extent to which they exhibit their control purpose. Nevertheless, it is significant that the vivid imagination of the early Christians lent itself to such use.

Beside the skilful utilization of the sanctions of reward and punishment, the willingness to undergo martyrdom was induced by a second factor, namely, by indoctrination through the use of sacred scriptures. Evidently it was a source of satisfaction to the martyr to reflect that his fate was so fully under the control of God that it had long ago been foretold. The thought that he was one of a noble company was tremendously effective, and he was conscious of his heroic status largely because he found himself to be in a situation similar to those celebrated in sacred story. In the same source were to be found many comforting exhortations, which, if known and heeded, would greatly assist him by pointing out the position gained by exemplary characters of the past, and promising him a like fame.

The Scriptures were consciously employed for this purpose. Even in the earlier situations, when there was no New Testament to be used, the Jewish writings readily lent themselves to the required use, especially in the Greek translation which was in common use among the Christians. These Scriptures, containing, for example, the stories of the Jewish martyrs of the Maccabean revolt, were widely quoted in the Christian literature of martyrdom. But in the times of the persecutions properly so called, the New Testament, with its stories of Paul and the teaching and the potent example of Jesus, furnished an even greater abundance of materials of which full advantage was taken.

It is therefore not surprising to read from Tertullian, who, though ardent, was at the same time a sagacious leader, that at any time when forewarning or reminiscence made it necessary, the Christians assembled to read their Scriptures (*Apology* 39). Elsewhere he proves from Scripture the duty and the usefulness of martyrdom (*ibid.* 20), and shows how God has willed and commanded it (*Scorpiace* 2). The range of such usage of sacred writing may be seen from his work; for example, a series of examples from Jewish sources is introduced by the formula, "Let the Gospels wait a little while I set forth their root in the Law"; then, after citations are made, the New Testament is likewise quoted after the formula, "It remains to review the modern Christian system" (*ibid.* 2, 9). Clement of Alexandria stresses especially the prophetic element in the sacred books; and from it by extensive quotation he similarly proves, at least to his own satisfaction, that martyrdom is taught. By him, again, the scriptural warrant is introduced by a stock formula: "Should you wish to be a martyr for the hope of advantage you shall hear again" (*Miscellanies* iv. 7). Perhaps even more instructive is his use of the teaching of Jesus for the same purpose: "On martyrdom the Lord has spoken explicitly, and what is written in different places we bring together . . . ."; and citations are made (*ibid.* iv. 9; cf. also iv. 6, 11).

As might be expected, the later churchmen, when the institutional value of Scripture was correspondingly magnified, were even more prolific in their use of it to induce an attitude of willingness to undergo martyrdom. For example, Cyprian rhetorically wrote to a persecutor: "Why does not your stricken and alienated mind perceive the lively remedies which we both learn and teach from the heavenly Scriptures?" (*Treatise* iii. 23).

Still more rhetorical is his statement to the effect that "when we read these things, and things of the like kind, brought together in the Gospel, and feel, as it were, torches placed under us, with the Lord's words to inflame our faith, we not only do not dread, but we even provoke the enemies of truth" (*ibid*. iii. 20). His treatise, *On Exhortation to Martyrdom*, is highly instructive in the range, amount, and method of its quotations. Another later writer is quite as explicit to the same effect, "Having before them all the examples and models and noble tokens which are given us in the divine and sacred Scriptures, the blessed martyrs who were with us did not hesitate, but . . . . they adhered firmly to their calling" (Eusebius *Church History* viii. 10. 2, 3).

A detail which is of importance in this connection is the memorization of Scripture texts, including the stories of martyrdom. Eusebius noted how greatly comforted was a group of banished confessors by the ability of one of their number, who, although as a part of his punishment he had been blinded, was able to quote widely from the Scriptures (*Martyrs of Palestine* xiii. 8). Cyprian remarked at the fitness of appointing a confessor to the office of Reader:

Nothing is more suitable for the voice which has confessed the Lord with a glorious utterance than to sound him forth in the solemn repetition of the divine lessons, than, after the sublime words which spoke out the witness for Christ, to read the gospel of Christ whence martyrs are made [*Epistle* xxii. 2; cf. xxxiii. 4].

Caution may perhaps warrant the notation that it is only the pragmatic effect of such use of Scripture which is emphasized. Doubtless in many instances of use the wish was father to the thought. It is not suggested that more was secured by this feature than the strengthening of an attitude which already had other elements as its basis. However, the formation within the church of a body of sacred writings, and the investiture of this corpus with institutional value, is an important feature of the development of ecclesiastical consciousness. As such, the rôle played in the control of Christians in situations of persecution was important, even though subordinate.

Indoctrination was effected not only through the use of Scripture but also by the discipline of church customs. It cannot be too forcibly stressed that the conflict of church and state was a conflict of loyalty to groups. The churches were religious societies, exactly as was the state in its attempt to secure religious conformity to approved patterns. To which society should the Christian affirm loyalty? Membership in the Christian group had appealed to him sufficiently to cause him to join it and to remain in fellowship up to the moment of his crisis. Presumably it had not only brought him satisfactions but had also left its mark upon him in teaching him certain manners and habits. Such factors, when perceived in connection with his as yet unbroken fellowship, strongly influenced him. Common worship, the association of the liturgy, particularly of the common liturgical meal, the practical benevolence practiced by the several societies, and all such social features, operated to unite the members into well-knit groups.

The force of such a relation is apparent in the crises through which the churches passed. It is apparent as fellowship was lost through denial. Much distress followed. The sources suggest that many of those who lacked the courage to confess nevertheless, immediately after defection, returned to their group beseeching restoration to fellowship. Many deniers resorted to the confessors in prison to beg "peace" from them. That in some cases the confessors acted upon the prestige which they had acquired through their persistence, and wrote certificates of pardon, furnished church officials with a problem, for the deniers, equipped with certificates, came to their churches and demanded restoration to rights. They evidently valued their fellowship, even though they lacked the courage to affirm it.

The effect of the discipline of custom is seen also in the operation of ritual. The withdrawal of the Eucharist, where most particularly dramatic communion was secured, was a serious matter to deniers. Doubtless in this central sacramental feature of the common worship there was considerable magical value for the devotee. But whatever may have been the motive in ascribing value to the rite, the social effect of its customary celebration is undoubted. It is equally obvious that it operated powerfully in the process of control.

But it was not only through the undirected influence of ecclesiastical rites that control was secured. Formal discipline was applied by the specific assertion of authority. The lay Christian looked with some awe to his officials. The bishop had the power to admit or to refuse the privileges of the church to deniers, and this very matter led to a serious dispute over a stricter and a more lenient point of view in the matter of securing control in persecution. Authority and the formal rights of the church, as well as the disciplinary effect of common custom, must be reckoned among the influences in the control of candidates for martyrdom.

The function of the group acting in church discipline may readily be exhibited. Tertullian graphically pictures a local situation, perhaps with more zeal than exactness:

When is trust in God more strong than when there is a greater fear of him, and persecution breaks out? The church is awestruck. Then is faith more zealous in preparation, and better disciplined in fasts, meetings, prayers, lowliness, brotherly kindness, and love, in holiness and temperance. There is no room, in fact, for aught but fear and hope [*Of Flight in Persecution* 1].

While this is a highly emotional reflection of what might have been desired in a time of persecution, doubtless the more practical leaders similarly recognized, with Cyprian, that "he cannot be fitted for martyrdom who is not armed for the contest by the church" (*Epistle* liii. 4), and saw to it that such arming was effected. Naturally, they first turned for its accomplishment to the common meeting:

That the day of our struggle is already approaching, we should not cease to be instant with all the people in fastings, in watchings, in prayers. Let us be urgent, with constant groanings and frequent prayers. For these are our heavenly arms, which make us to stand fast and bravely to persevere. These are the spiritual defenses and divine weapons which defend us [Cyprian *ibid*. lvi. 5].

The influence of the Eucharist has been mentioned. In further detail it may be said that, as it early became useful to cite the example of Jesus as martyr, it was found that a powerful mode of doing this was by its dramatic representation through the ritual. Not only was there thus presented a model, but the process was accompanied by a high content of emotional value. Presently a magical value was thought also to be inherent.

These factors may be observed in the sources. For instance, "A severer and a fiercer fight is now threatening, for which the soldiers of Christ ought to prepare themselves with uncorrupted faith and robust courage, considering that they drink the cup of Christ's blood daily"—thus Cyprian (*ibid*. lv. 1).

Tertullian likewise testifies to the effectiveness of the rite: "We are called to the warfare of the living God in our very response to the sacramental words" (*To the Martyrs* 3). In another source Cyprian calls attention to a case of successful control: "Those lips sanctified by heavenly food after the body and blood of the Lord have rejected the profane contacts and the leavings of the idols" (*Treatise* iii. 2), while failure is indignantly reproached in the same figure; certain lapsed persons are said to have "forsaken the Lord's bread and cup to hasten freely to a profane contract" (*ibid.* iii. 7). In the same vein he insists that "his spirit is deficient which the Eucharist received does not raise and stimulate" (*Epistle* liii. 4). The confessors, he stated, could not abide the idolatrous rites; "Their lips, hallowed with food divine, could not endure, after the body and blood of the Lord, the food that remained over from the feasts" (*Treatise* iii. 8).

Another particular item in the preparation of martyrs by the discipline of church custom was the emotional influence of song. It was noted in several successful cases of martyrdom that the heroes received comfort and confirmation of purpose through this means, obviously acquired in their church association. Perpetua sang psalms (*Martyrdom of SS. Perpetua and Felicitas* vi. 1). Pionius and his associates met their prison experiences with continued glorias (*Acts of Pionius and His Associates* xi. 6), while the martyrs of Palestine "sang and offered up hymns and thanksgivings to the God of the Universe till their very last breath" (Eusebius *Church History* viii. 9. 5).

With reference to the direct extension of control by authority, while it is evident that when the issue appeared authority was asserted, the degree of success is not evident. Certainly the churches were embarrassed by the fact that some of the bishops were themselves unable to perform that which they commanded their flocks to do. Not only did a number of bishops lapse and deny their faith (Cyprian *Treatise* iii. 6; *Epistle* lxiii. 1; lxvii. 6), but others compromised themselves by flight in order to avoid court proceedings (*Life and Passion of Cyprian* 7, 8, 11). While the attempt was made to dignify their behavior by calling flight withdrawal, retirement, or banishment, nevertheless the bishop so situated had difficulty in maintaining the authority of his office. However, the assertion of authority was attempted, with some measure of success, at least.

That the most strategic attempts in persecution made specific aim at the clergy and officials indicates that their authority was recognized by the state to be effective. On the other hand, the failure of such efforts clearly suggests that formal authority was not the most important element in winning the issue.

An instructive aspect of the question of formal authority was the situation broached by the appeals of the lapsed members for readmission to the churches on the basis of certificates from confessors

(Cyprian *Epistle* x; xv; xvi; xvii). The rulings of the bishops were not uniformly accepted; indeed, to some of the lapsed, and to some of the churches also, the certificate of an imprisoned confessor was more authoritative than the law of a hiding bishop. But the bishops had their following, also; and ultimately they won their point.

The clearest evidence of the social value of church discipline appears from the disorganization which resulted as persecution or local suppression entailed the interruption of meetings. Regular meetings of the societies were held as long as possible; but presently this became an element of danger, since it marked out to the opponents of the Christians where their victims might be found (Cyprian *ibid.* iv. 2) and aided in identifying Christians as such. Meetings were then abandoned, or held surreptitiously and at irregular intervals. This led to considerable confusion. The sacramental services were interrupted; instruction was not being offered to the catechumens; and there lacked the encouragement of fellowship and unity (Tertullian *Scorpiace* 2). A particularly vital problem was the fate of the partially instructed catechumens (Cyprian *Epistle* xii; lxxii. 22).

Further, there is abundant evidence that willingness to undergo martyrdom depended largely upon the strength of the social contact of the confessor with his church. This appears indubitably from the fact that martyrdom away from the home associations was held by Christian leaders to be less desirable than the public death of a martyr in the sight of his fellows (*ibid*. lxxvi).

Another factor involving matters of discipline was the special position of the confessors. It was only natural that the example and exhortation of a confessor should be effective; they had actually passed their first crisis and were awaiting probable death. Consequently their influence was great. But it was this very influence which became an embarrassment to the duly authorized officials, when the imprisoned confessors assumed, as they seldom did, to declare peace to the lapsed, and in an almost curt tone to inform their bishop (whom they sometimes had the temerity to address as *frater* rather than as *papa*) that they had done so (*ibid*. xvi; xviii; xlix). A courageous bishop like Cyprian had to write in turn that the authority of a confessor, though deservedly great, was less than that of his bishop, and to direct that confessors were not to confer certificates of peace except as they were directed, subject to their bishop, to do so (*ibid*. ix; xvii; xix; xxix; liv. 13).

The problem of the lapsed members greatly disturbed the social function of the churches. In such a persecution as that of Decius thousands renounced their faith and performed the required sacrifices. But of these, many soon after sought readmission to their broken fellowship (Cyprian *ibid*. xx. 2). What to do with them was a problem, of magnitude, since the number was large, and of kind, since differing policies presently appeared.

Stricter and milder standards were considered. Indeed, a schism of some importance occurred over the point, Novatian taking the more lenient position (Cyprian *ibid*. li) while Cyprian insisted that the lapsed persons might not be readmitted except after repentance, probation, and duly supervised penance (*Treatise* iii; *On the Lapsed*). However, numerous exceptions were made to the more rigorous ruling, and a general decree of readmission seems to have been promulgated (Cyprian *Epistle* lii).

It may thus be said with confidence that whether operating with a degree of informality or in organized purpose in ritual and authoritative discipline, the social control over candidates for martyrdom was effected by the Christian societies. In all forms of such activity the churches acted as social agencies. Operating as groups, a sufficient impression of the value of their fellowship was generated that they were highly efficient in attaining their objectives. The basic element in the control of their adherents was the force of the value of unity. It was for the maintenance of the unity that rewards were promised, and for the failure to maintain it that punishment was threatened. Both the rewards and the punishments were asserted, and knowledge of them gained, through the fellowship which must be kept inviolate. The martyrs were prepared in their fellowship as a Christian society, which, through meetings, ritual, and authority, succeeded in producing the necessary attitudes of which its martyrs were made.

III

THE PRODUCTION OF ATTITUDES

From the range and definiteness of the reward
and punishment imagery, it may be inferred with
certainty that the fellowship of prospective martyrs
in their church groups functioned to prepare the
witness for his fate. The effectiveness of his fellowship is further apparent in the place which ritualistic practices filled in sending him to his experience
impelled by the dramatic representation of a gloriously accomplished victory. Obviously these, together with the reinforcing examples and exhortations learned from Scripture, were results of the
social contacts of groups. Add to these the formal
authority of ecclesiastical organization, and it becomes apparent that the religious societies functioned with considerable power in the preparation
of the martyr.

Cases of martyrdom were successful largely because of the candidate's readiness. This readiness
was secured by a process of thorough preparation,
which was effected, as has been pointed out, by the
social function of church groups. The process consisted of the skilful use of the sanctions of reward
and punishment, disciplines of social custom, cere-
monial, and exhortation, and, as shall presently be
shown, by the representation of attitudes which
made the behavior of the candidate conform to type.

The effort of the state, as has been seen, was by threat or inducement to cause the suspected or accused Christian to forsake his loyalty to a disapproved religious group. Correspondingly, it was the necessity of the Christian group to maintain the loyalties which had been built up. Since the legal processes were generally the same in successive actions, the attempt to meet them was possible, and it was made.

The goal of the church groups, as general practice became typical, was to anticipate whatever event might ensue in the relations between the state and Christians. Uniformity of behavior was desirable; if each witness might be taught to do exactly what his predecessors had done, the possibility of failure to confess would be much reduced. Failure, when it occurred, came when the witness was unprepared, had not undergone the discipline of normative custom, or was faced by some unforeseen circumstance which impaired the uniformity of the course of events.

What was aimed at was to make the conduct of the witness in every eventuality *predictable*, for the predictable is always controllable; if it is not possible to control the event, the attitude toward it may be controlled. The Christians might not prevent persecution; but they might, and did, control the behavior of those affected by it.

The mode of control was essentially the same as that of any group influence: by a certain type of education to build up a set of attitudes. The hope was that when the suspect or accused was brought before the authorities he would not be taken by surprise, and thus be at a loss for his answers, nor be under the necessity of conducting himself totally according to the exigencies of an unknown situation. The churches undertook to formulate the loyalties of their adherents, not leaving the matter to chance. They stated in exact terms what that loyalty was and what it implied. They attempted to supply the exact directions by which each step in the legal procedure might be met. They recommended answers to the judge's questions, and framed replies to the arguments of state officials. They even held the attention of witnesses during their examinations. Finally, they attempted so to control witnesses that if their cases issued adversely they would prefer martyrdom to release by denial. All these steps in the production of attitudes may be seen in specific cases.

In the first place, the answers to the question of guilt were centrally important. The witness must admit that he was a Christian. Consequently, as the acts of the martyrs were published, one sees the skilful use which was made of the court dialogue. By circulating representations of the cases of successful witness, and in them citing the questions asked by the court and the answers given by the confessor, the first necessity, namely, that of suggesting the proper answer to the question of guilt, was met.

Among the best, and significantly, the earliest,

examples are the stories of Justin and of the Scillitan martyrs. Justin's answer is reiterated: "I am a Christian." The abstract of the court proceeding in which the Scillitan martyrs were condemned is more detailed: "Vestian said, 'I am a Christian.' Speratus said, 'I am a Christian,' and with him all agreed. Speratus said again, 'I am a Christian,' and with him all agreed."

Other pious responses were cited. It was said that Cyprian wished to be put to death while in the very act of speaking about God (*Life and Passion of Cyprian* 14). The custom of reiterating the answer under torture is noted by Tertullian:

We say, and before all men we say, and torn and bleeding under torture we cry out, "We worship God through Christ," "God is great and good," "Which may God give," are the words on every lip. It bears witness that God is judge, exclaiming, "God sees!" and, "I commend myself to God!" and "God will repay me" [*Apology* 17, 21].

A remarkable instance of uniform response is alleged of a notably successful martyrdom described in the letter of the Christians of Lyons and Vienne:

Sanctus, while the wicked men hoped by torture to wring something from him which he ought not to say, would not even tell his name, nation, or city, but answered in the Roman tongue to all the questions, "I am a Christian," and the people heard from him no other word. . . . . They heard from Sanctus no other word than the confession which he had uttered from the beginning [Eusebius *Church History* v. 1. 20].

Similarly Tertullian notes that upon apprehension "I am a Christian," the man cries out (*Apology*

2). Cyprian cites the common response: "But now, when of my own free will I confess, and cry out, and with words frequent and repeated and to the same effect bear witness that I am a Christian . . . . (*Treatise* v. 13). There is a long list of "Acts of Martyrdom" in which the uniform response is cited.[1]

There is a hint that a certain posture during the examination was thought to be especially effective. Thus Tertullian: "Then, too, in using such words as these, it [i.e., the soul] looks not to the Capitol, but to the heavens. It knows that there is the throne of the living God, as from him and from thence itself came down" (*Apology* 17).

Certainly it was believed that to make the sign of the cross was efficacious. Tertullian affirms, "We trace upon the forehead the sign" (*On the Crown* 3), and in another place says, "We have faith for our defense, if we are not smitten with distrust also, in immediately making the sign of the cross and adjuring" (*Scorpiace* 1). The phrase, "so many confessors sealed with a second inscription upon their brows," occurs in the story of Cyprian (*Life and Passion of Cyprian* 7). The instance is given of one standing in the form of the cross: "A youth not twenty years of age standing unbound and stretching out his hands in the form of a cross, with untrembling and unterrified mind, earnestly engaged

[1] *Passion of S. Pionius* 9; *Acts of S. Cyprian* 1; *Passion of S. Boniface* 8; *Acts of S. Saturninus* 8, 16; *Acts of S. Didymus* 1; *Acts of S. Tarachus* 1, 2, 3; *Acts of S. Basil of Ancyra*, 3, 5.

in prayer to God" (Eusebius *Church History* viii. 7. 4). It will be remembered that one item figuring among the causes of Diocletian's persecution was the interference with the consultation of the omens by Christians making the sign of the cross (Lactantius *Death of the Persecutors* 10).

The definiteness of these attitudes and the specificity of their functioning were secured by maintaining a degree of fixity of attention upon the end so ardently desired. This prevented the intrusion of unprepared-for eventualities. Control, as is well known, is obtained largely by the focus of attention being fixed upon a given point. The Christian groups maintained, with a high degree of success, such a fixation of attention upon the values which it was thought would lead to the behavior deemed proper.

Of this element in the process of control there are many examples. As early a source as the letter of Clement of Rome, which probably reflects a situation of temporary tensity, contains the significant exhortation: "Let us fix our eyes upon the blood of Christ" (I Clem. 7). "Let us attend to what is good, pleasing, and acceptable. . . . . Let us look stedfastly to the blood of Christ" (*ibid.*). Polycarp cited particular models: "I exhort you all . . . . to exercise all patience, such as you have seen before your eyes, not only in the case of the blessed Ignatius and Zozimus and Rufus, but also in others among yourselves, and in Paul himself and the rest of the apostles" (*Epistle of Polycarp* 9).

In the events described in the story of Polycarp's martyrdom it is alleged that "some even reached such a pitch of nobility that none of them groaned or wailed, showing to all of us that at the hour of their torture the noble martyrs of Christ were absent from the flesh, or, rather, that the Lord was standing by and talking with them" (*Martyrdom of Polycarp* ii. 2). The explanation of this which the source offers is that "they set before their eyes an escape from the fire which is everlasting and never quenched, and with the eyes of their heart they looked up to the good things which are preserved for those who have endured" (*ibid*. ii. 3).

Such a fixation is alleged also in one of the Lyons and Vienne martyrs: "Alexander neither groaned nor murmured in any manner, but communed in his heart with God" (Eusebius *Church History* v. 1. 52). It is remarked that "the leg does not feel the chain when the mind is in the heavens" (Tertullian *To the Martyrs* 2). It was a proper insight which recommended candidates to "think less of death than of immortality" and which insisted that "it behooves us to embrace these things in our mind and consideration and meditate on these things day and night," for it was sensibly observed that "the brave and stedfast mind founded on religious meditations endures, and the spirit abides unmoved against all the terrors of the devil and the threats of the world, when it is strengthened by the sure and solid faith of things to come" (Cyprian *Epistle* viii. 2; *Treatise* xi. 13). The sources abound with examples which base such practical advice upon sound observation.

The discussion of the attitudes which controlled the martyrs necessitates the recognition that in part, at any rate, they were of a psychopathic character. It hardly needs to be said that the experience of martyrdom was one against which ordinary judgment recoils. It will occasion no surprise, then, to find that in cases of martyrdom certain symptoms of a psychosis appear. One finds, for example, a morbid desire for the experience of martyrdom. Even though it may be rationalized that the desire was so keen because of the rewards which were expected to materialize, the affirmation may be offered that the desire was morbid. In the phenomena there appear, too, evidences that there was a morbid pleasure derived from the pains which were endured. Indeed, it seems that martyrdom in the later church occupied the place which in the earlier church was filled by such ecstatic experiences as trance and speaking in tongues. There is a definitely discoverable basis for such phenomena.

In the first place, that there was a morbid desire for martyrdom is evident from Christian sources, some of which encourage and others of which condemn the attitude, and from non-Christian sources as well. Ignatius of Antioch exhibited a hotly ardent desire for the death which awaited him in Rome, writing in advance of his arrival to make sure that the Roman Christians would not disappoint his wish by securing his release (Ignatius *To the Romans* iv. 8). Pothinus of the Lyons and Vienne group earnestly desired martyrdom (Eusebius *Church History* v. 1. 30). Others of this group "besought the brethren with tears that earnest prayers should be offered that they might be made perfect" (i.e., die as well as confess [*ibid.* v. 2. 3]). Tertullian claims that "we shrink not from the grapple with your utmost rage, coming forth even of our own accord to the contest, and condemnation gives us more pleasure than acquittal" (*To Scapula* 1). He further says that "these things [i.e., sword, wild beasts, crucifixion, fire, and torture] have been calmly endured by many, and have even been eagerly desired for the sake of fame and glory, and this not only in the case of men but of women, too" (*To the Martyrs* 4).

Perhaps as instructive a case of pathological attitudes as may be cited is that of Origen, who, it will be remembered, in no other features was characterized by such a volatile disposition as that represented by Tertullian, but who, on the contrary was intellectually one of the finest minds in the rank of Christian leaders. It is related that in the persecution of Decius, with a rash boldness he thrust himself before the attention of the state officials, eagerly courting arrest and martyrdom. Failing because of his youth to win his desire, he determined to offer himself at the court. But his plan was checkmated by the simple expedient of his mother, who prevented his appearance in public by hiding his clothing, for such was the curious attitude of Origen that he who was eager to die could not entertain the thought of indecent exposure. When his father was apprehended in the same persecution the youth wrote him a letter reciting reasons why he should maintain his confession, and urging him not to let the ties of affection for mother and child deter him from the glorious fate of martyrdom. The same frame of mind may be seen in Origen's *Exhortation to Martyrdom*, and, in its most extreme expression, his act of self-emasculation.

The more sober judgments about voluntarily offering one's self also witness to the presence of pathological desire. In as early a source as the story of Polycarp the failure of one who had offered himself is made the basis of the notation that "we do not commend those who give themselves up, since the Gospel does not give this teaching" (*Martyrdom of Polycarp* 4). Clement of Alexandria agreed with this position, saying, "He who presents himself before the judgment seat becomes guilty of his death. And such is the case of him who does not avoid persecution, but out of daring presents himself for capture . . . . if he uses provocation he is wholly guilty" (*Miscellanies* iv. 10). He elsewhere says, "There are some not belonging to us, but sharing the name merely, who are in haste to give themselves up" (*ibid*. iv. 3). Commodianus notes the presence of those who desire martyrdom, but aligns himself with those who took the temperate view (*Instructions* 6).

What is important in the present connection is

that these judgments establish the fact of a contrary point of view and demonstrate that the pathological desire for martyrdom had considerable currency. It will of course be remembered that not all
Christian leaders took the negative attitude toward voluntary surrender. The extreme statements
of Tertullian will be recalled, even though they
must be discounted. The view of Cyprian will be
taken even more seriously. More significant, and
less open to the question of fact, are the several
known cases of willing surrender.

Furthermore, it was not among Christian groups
only that the morbid desire for martyrdom was
noted. Non-Christians recognized it also. "We are
accounted a desperate, reckless race," said Tertullian (*Apology* 50), who also cites common nick-
names which reflect the reputation by which certain Christians, at least, were known: "Call us, if
you like, *Sarmenticii* and *Semaxii*, because, bound
to the half-axle stake, we are burned in a circle heap
of faggots" (*ibid.*). Obviously, the currency of so
common a reputation that it was caricatured witnesses that the attitude which was basic to it was
widespread. Marcus Aurelius refers to the attitude:
"The soul should be ready at any moment to be
separated from the body, but this readiness must
come from a man's own calm judgment, not from
mere obstinacy and a tragic show, as with the
Christians" (*Meditations* xi. 3).

But the most telling recognition of such an attitude is the fact that it was satirized. The clever

Lucian did not fail to observe the Acts of Martyrdom literature, as may be seen from his story of the behavior of Proteus Peregrinus during his Christian period:

Proteus having been arrested for that [i.e., being a Christian], was thrown into prison. That sufficed to procure for him during the rest of his life a great authority, and he valued the reputation to have performed miracles. . . . . Why, these poor wretches have persuaded themselves that they are going to be every whit immortal and live forever, wherefore they both despise death and voluntarily devote themselves to it—the most of them [*Of the Death of Peregrinus* 11–13].

One of the elements of the morbid desire for martyrdom was the abnormal enjoyment of the pain which it involved. This phenomenon is known as "masochism." Certain persons, who because of their possession of the tendency are usually adjudged to be abnormal, derive pleasure from the pain which they themselves suffer. The phenomenon is of general manifestation; perhaps the best illustration of it is the flagellants of the Middle Ages. It is the counterpart of sadism, the behavior in which pleasure is derived from the infliction of pain upon others. Clearly the voluntary surrender of one's self to the experience of martyrdom, when it was known that the most exquisite tortures were involved, is *prima facie* evidence of the presence of the tendency toward masochism. When certain cases exhibit more than the willingness to undertake the experience, but even an insatiable desire to force it, the fact becomes unquestionable.

It has been well said,

We have what seems to be satisfactory evidence that not only strong men but even delicate and sensitive women exhibited the power of inhibiting the normal reactions to the most excruciating torments. This almost incredible power of inhibition can only be explained as the result of the building up of a pathologically intense, ecstatic mental state. . . . . The masochistic phenomena are the most remarkable characteristic of the early martyrdoms, and if a collection were made of the masochistic passages of the writings . . . . the bulk of them would be . . . . great.[1]

A brief selection of such passages brings to light the presence of the attitude in numerous cases. For example, it was the highly intellectual Clement of Alexandria who discouraged voluntary surrender, who nevertheless wrote that "the same rule holds with pains, some of which we endure, and others we shun. . . . . The martyr chooses the pleasure which exists in prospect through the present pain" (*Miscellanies* iv. 9).

Tertullian's enthusiasm may account for much of the sweeping quality of his statements, but they represent at least a certain element of the Christian public. Speaking of the willingness to undertake martyrdom, he says of the Christian that "if he is pointed out he glories in it, if he is accused he makes no defense, interrogated he makes voluntary confession, condemned he renders thanks" (*Apology* 1). "We who so willingly yield ourselves to the sword"

[1] Edwards, *The Transformation of Early Christianity from an Eschatological to a Social Movement* (Menasha, Wisconsin, 1919), p. 21.

is his characterization of the Christian (*ibid.* 37), while he affirms that "we rejoice to be counted as his [Christ's] disciples, and in his name to suffer" (*ibid.* 21).

The same leader goes so far as to say that "the spirit . . . . incites all almost to go and offer themselves in martyrdom, not to flee from it" (*Of Flight in Persecution* 9), and with slight equivocation implies that pleasure is derived from the experience: "We do not shrink from the grapple with your utmost rage, coming forth even of our own accord to the contest, and condemnation gives us more pleasure than acquittal" (*To Scapula* 1).

But Tertullian's frankest statement is this:

The flesh, perhaps, will dread the merciless sword, and the lofty cross, and the rage of wild beasts, and the punishment of the flames—of all most terrible—and all the skill of the executioner in torture. But, on the other side, let the spirit set clearly before both itself and the flesh how these things, though exceedingly painful, have yet been calmly endured by many [*To the Martyrs* 4].

A certain discount necessitated by characteristic overstatement must also be made in reading the writings of Cyprian. Even so, however, their value in the present connection is not altogether vitiated. Their evidence is to the same effect as that already found to have characterized Christians of other localities: "The combat has increased, and the glory of the combatants has increased also. Nor were you kept back from the struggle by fear of tortures, but by the tortures themselves you were more and more stimulated to the conflict" (*Epistle* viii). The morbid attitude is but thinly veiled when he writes, "When we read of these things, and things of the like kind brought together in the Gospel, and feel, as it were, torches placed under us, we not only do not dread, but we even provoke the enemies of faith" (*ibid.* xxv). The pathological quality is unmistakable as he rhetorically asks, "What is more blessed . . . . than to have begun to love one's punishments after having faith to bear them" (*ibid.*). Finally, he frankly urges that "this thing [i.e., martyrdom] is to be embraced and desired" (*Treatise* xi. 4).

Eusebius refers to some cases of martyrdom in the later persecutions in which masochistic phenomena appear. One of them is an instance in which "six young men . . . . went in haste . . . . evidencing great zeal for martyrdom. They confessed . . . . and by their ambition for all terrible things they showed that they who glory in the religion of the God of the Universe do not cower before the attacks of wild beasts" (*Martyrs of Palestine* iii. 3). Another case implies in so extreme a form of voluntary surrender an approach to the masochistic urge:

And regarding with indifference the terrible things and the multiform tortures, they declared themselves boldly and undauntedly. . . . . They received the final sentence of death with joy and laughter and cheerfulness, so that they sang and offered up hymns and thanksgivings . . . . till their very last breath [*Church History* viii. 9. 5].

Were further evidence necessary it would be forthcoming in the frankness, not to say delight, with which the tortures of the martyrs were recounted. To be sure, this is an attitude largely conditioned by the time and place of the composition of the martyrological literature. That is to say, it is a convention which is no longer current. This fact should caution against laying too much weight upon the factor. Doubtless it was not regarded in such a light by the writers and the public of the martyrologies. However, the detail with which the death of Polycarp is described, or the revolting features of the torture of Blandina, allows the inference to be drawn. An even more compelling example is constituted by the pathetic items of the family relations in the story of SS. Perpetua and Felicitas, for in this story such details are related for the obvious purpose of exciting an emotional response. Whatever discount must be made from these typical stories, the details of torture in the later martyrologies are so unnecessarily explicit that they unmistakably reveal the pleasure which accrued to writer and reader in the contemplation of pain. The masochistic phenomena are obvious.

To be sure, the presence of masochistic phenomena in the literature of martyrdom indicates that it was doubtless the authors who wrote and the public who read it who shared perhaps most largely the pleasure from pain. But to say this is only in another direction to emphasize the control purpose of the literature. Such function is readily capable of

generalization; it has a survival value.[1] To celebrate
the exploits of a suffering hero, or to picture the
personified torture of an idealized institution may,
and in the cases of the Acts of Martyrdom unquestionably did, have a profound effect in inducing
others to accept a share of the responsibility of aid.

There is another set of abnormal phenomena in
the behavior of the martyrs, even less pleasant to
discuss. The sexual behavior of imprisoned confessors was an item which figured in the total of their
attitudes. Its implications may be seen in several
features. The fact that women as well as men were
persecuted, together with the fact that the persecution of women often involved shameful treatment,
ranging from indecent exposure to enforced prosti-
tution, suggests the relation of the sexual feature so
far as women were concerned. That the usual
treatment of women was not thoroughly efficient
as a deterrent raises the question whether an abnormal sexual attitude must not be investigated
with other items making up the martyr psychosis.

The data are various. One matter of less, though
of not inconsiderable, importance, was the custom
of the kiss in greeting confessors. This, too, was a
convention quite common in the time and place
of the early Christians. It was quite usual to go
to the prisons, obtain access to the confessors by
bribing the jailors, and then in ministering to the
wants of the confessors to exchange the kiss. Eusebius notes that Origen, unusually emotional in this

[1] Edwards, *op. cit.*, p. 21.

respect, rashly exposed himself to danger when he with extreme boldness saluted the holy martyrs with a kiss (*Church History* vi. 6. 3, 4). Cyprian wrote to a group of confessors, "What [is] more pleasant and sublime than now to kiss your lips, which with a glorious voice have confessed the Lord?" (*Epistle* lxxx. 1). With still greater emotion he wrote in a formal treatise, "We look with glad countenances upon confessors illustrious with the heraldry of a good name and glorious with the praise of virtue and faith; clinging to them with holy kisses, we embrace them long desired with insatiable eagerness" (*Treatise* iii. 2). Eusebius notes as a typical case that of "Theodosia, a faithful and sedate maiden, not yet eighteen years of age," who "went up to certain prisoners who were confessing the kingdom of Christ and sitting before the judgment seat, and saluted them" (*Martyrs of Palestine* vii. 1).

Now, had this custom not been abused, nothing might properly be said about it. The modern may not with justice object to a convention which was quite innocently regarded by those among whom it was current. It would be comparable to that convention which, however, proves to be embarrassing to those among whom it is not customary, of saluting with a kiss the hero upon whom a military medal is conferred. But that the kiss of confessors carried in certain cases less innocent implications also clearly appears from the fact that contemporaries found it objectionable.

Homosexuality is, of course, implied. But in some cases which involved opposite sexes the abuse of the kiss appears to have led to behavior which met with disapproval. Tertullian calls attention to the jealousy of the non-Christian husband of a Christian wife in the matter: "He will not allow her to be absent all night long at nocturnal convocations and paschal solemnities, nor even suffer her to creep into a prison to kiss a martyr's bonds, or even to exchange a kiss with one of the brethren" (*To Wives* ii. 4. 5). Other evidence of the abuse of the ritual kiss is obtainable;[1] in the situation of Cyprian the abuse had specific reference to the sexual behavior of certain imprisoned confessors, so that Cyprian had explicitly to denounce their disgraceful sexual relationship (*Epistle* v. 3; vii. 5).

Still another factor suggests additional data of a sexual element in the martyr psychosis. The kiss was sublimated in thought until one of the rewards of confession was the kiss of the martyr by the heavenly Christ. This formed one of the items of the sanction of reward. For example, Saturus, in the story of SS. Perpetua and Felicitas, in a vision received Christ's kiss (*Passion of SS. Perpetua and Felicitas* iv. 2). Cyprian urged that martyrdom would bring one to the embrace and the kiss of Christ (*On the Lapsed* 2; *Epistle* xxxvii), and wrote to certain women that one inviting prospect of their

[1] Clement of Alexandria *The Pedagogue* 3:11; Athenagoras *A Plea for the Christians* 32; Tertullian *Apology* 39.

martyrdom was that they should come to the kiss
and the embrace of the Lord (*Epistle* lxxx).

As in other matters, it is the recognition of these
phenomena by non-Christians which the more
strongly establishes their significance. Of course,
the same critical examination is to be made of their
statements as is made of those by Christians.
Nevertheless, it is noteworthy that the sexual implications of persecution were noticed by these and
discussed in their writings. Doubtless the oft-
alleged accusation of incest, which was apparently
one of the most effective of the charges against the
Christians, rested merely upon misunderstanding
resulting from secrecy and upon maliciously spread
reports. But the explicit notice of sexual irregulari-
ties which was made by the satirist Lucian cannot
lightly be passed over, for, even as satire, it suggests
the basis in fact which was being satirized. In the
well-known story of Peregrinus it is said that when
the release of the dubious hero was found to be impossible, the Christians "all the time zealously rendered him ministries of every sort. From earliest
dawn aged widows and orphan children were to be
seen waiting at the door of the prison, and men of
rank among them even obtained the privilege of
sleeping with him within by bribing the prison
guards" (*Of the Death of Peregrinus* 11–13).

Still another set of abnormal phenomena, but in
this case of quite a different quality, came through
the extreme veneration with which the martyrs
were held. They were indeed placed in the apostolic

succession, and the abilities of the apostles were ascribed to them. One of the most valued of these, which was ascribed from an early date, was the charism of prophecy. The thought that the martyr obtained this special power had great effect, it would appear, in inducing candidates to undertake the experience. They were assured that by doing so they would achieve the status of prophet. This is true in as early a case as the action against the group in which Polycarp was the most conspicuous figure. Of the martyrs on this occasion, it was said that they were sustained by visions of the rewards which were "shown by the Lord to them who were no longer men but already angels" (*Martyrdom of Polycarp* ii. 3). Polycarp was said to have had highly significant visions, by virtue of which he was called an "apostolic and prophetic teacher" (*ibid.* v. 12. 3; xvi. 12). Of the heroes of the Lyons and Vienne group, one, Attalus, was said to have had a notable vision (Eusebius *Church History* v. 3. 1–3; v. 7). It is important that the ascriptions of prophetic power developed so early.

The claim of the gift of vision and prophecy was, as might be expected, common among the Montanists. These Christians so highly prized this form of spiritistic behavior that they came to be regarded as eccentric. It is therefore not surprising that in the stories of martyrdom which reflect the experiences of members of this group there is emphasis upon the visionary element. The most representative example is the highly emotional story of the martyrdom of SS. Perpetua and Felicitas. The Preface to this work explicitly avows, "We . . . . both acknowledge and reverence, even as we do prophecies, modern visions equally promised us." The expectation aroused by so frank a statement is realized in several visions alleged of the persons of the story. The effectiveness of the factor among the Montanists is to be generalized in the fact that martyrdoms were reputed to be more than usually common among them.

However, it was not solely the fanatical sectaries who found persecution and martyrdom to be stimuli to visionary activity. Even the temperate bishop Dionysius based his withdrawal from persecution upon divine direction (Eusebius *Church History* vi. 40. 1). Eusebius mentions several cases of visions in connection with martyrdom (*ibid*. vi. 5. 5–7). Cyprian explicitly claimed the gift for confessors:

For this reason the divine rebuke does not cease to chastise us night and day. For besides the visions of the night, by day also the innocent age of boys is among us filled with the holy spirit, seeing in an esctasy with their eyes, and hearing and speaking those things whereby the Lord condescends to warn and instruct us [*Epistle* ix. 4].

In common estimation, therefore, a confessor who also enjoyed the rank of bishop was in an extraordinary position: "For whatever, in that moment of confession, the confessor-bishop speaks, he speaks in the mouth of all, by inspiration of God" (Cyprian *ibid*. lxxxii. 1). Not infrequently visions were alleged by Cyprian (*ibid*. xxxiii. 1; lxix. 10), and in the later martyrologies they are common.[1]

The question of the validity of such vision-experiences is not raised in the present connection. It is not in point. What is relevant is that they were alleged of confessors and martyrs; whether correctly or falsely does not matter, inasmuch as the significance of their ascription was their usefulness in control. As in the relation of heroic stories with masochistic detail, the matter of importance was the effect upon the reader. It was of value in inducing the attitude of willingness to undertake martyrdom to assure a potential martyr that he would, through his experience, achieve the rôle of prophet. It is probable that the inclusion of stories of vision-experiences in the literature of martyrdom was chiefly for the control purpose. As has been suggested in other matters, it is likely that several features of the experience of persecution filled the place in the latter church which spiritistic and ecstatic behavior occupied in the earlier church. Obviously the type of behavior represented by visions and prophecy is an example.

It may therefore be generalized that attitudes of a high degree of definiteness were induced in those who successfully undertook the difficult experience of confession and martyrdom. As it became possible, by reason of the frequency and the general uniformity of the anti-Christian actions, to know what

[1] Cf., for example, *Acts of John* 108; *Passion of S. Montanus* 21; *Passion of S. Theodoret* 8.

behavior was necessary on the part of the martyrs, it became increasingly possible to frame and teach the typical patterns. It became possible to suggest to those who faced the issue not only the information which would be useful but also the manners of procedure which had been found to be worthy of imitation. In many cases there was a pathological basis for such representation. But even when the symptoms of a psychosis are not apparent, the useful attitudes were in numerous cases induced. As the churches learned that their task was to secure a confession, it learned the process by which its task might be discharged. Events proved that the influence of the Christian fellowship was equal to its necessity.

IV

THE INFLUENCE OF THE GROUP

It has been suggested that in the actions of the state against the Christians, from which martyrs were made, the elements are capable of analysis as the function of group loyalties in situations where conflict raised the issue of control. The state, operating as a religious force with the backing of official and common social approval, was the party of the first part. The local churches, also religious groups, but suffering the disapproval of the state and the general public, were a conflicting party. In the issue which was precipitated it was the goal of the state to break down the loyalty of Christian adherents to the groups of their illegal allegiance; while, conversely, it was the task of the Christian societies to maintain that loyalty, even in the face of state opposition.

In the maintenance of its group integrity the action of a Christian church, collectively or in the person of its leaders, developed a readily analyzable process of control. Christians who were brought to a state court and presented with the alternative of confessing or denying the fact of their membership in an illegal society were subject to a degree of control by the group to which they belonged. In many cases they had been effectively prepared for the issue which faced them. They brought to it a balanced evaluation of the result of doing what was approved by the state and the general public or of doing what was desired by the group of the more immediately felt association. Rewards or punishments, sanctions or inhibitions, obedience to the ideal or acquiescence with the actual—all were alternatives which had been considered for them if not by them. There were definite attitudes to be taken, and not infrequently they had already been induced in the suspect. The outcome depended in large proportion upon the extent of the influence of the group of the immediate fellowship and upon the ability of the group to maintain its influence in the face of the counterinfluence of the state.

How far did the influence of the Christian group extend? It has already been pointed out that belonging to the Christian group had taught the prospective martyr the values to be gained through martyrdom. It had made him conscious of the rewards accruing, or, on the other hand, of the punishments which followed denial. If the resolution to confess had been, or had become, feeble, membership in the group strengthened it. Leaders had learned what must be done as the state carried out the steps of its examination, and lay members had been taught what was expected of them. Membership had effectually prepared the martyr for his experience, had in many cases produced the proper attitudes, and had fixed his attention upon the desired goal.

All this had been accomplished before the legal

processes took place. It is important to observe that the influence of the group, effective before, continued during the examination and even after confession or denial had been made. Finally, by recourse to manners of thought which were especially characteristic of the time and place, the area of influence was extended into the life which it was firmly believed would continue after the martyr had died in his faith.

Important as the postlegal extension of the influence of the group must have been, the crux of the entire matter lay in the more immediate expression of the influence of the group as the accused Christian had to meet his trial at law. True as it was that the readiness with which martyrs endured their bitter experience was the result of preparation, of the production of attitudes, and of the fixation of attention, it is equally true that the crucial moment was that moment when the witness was at the very tribunal. Even though he had been assured of special favor after he had made his confession, the confession must first be made. Granting the powerful appeal of the knowledge that after his death he would be venerated to the verge of worship, the fact of death was terrible. It is easy to suppose that, however well prepared one might be, or however strong may have been his resolution to confess, the terror of that moment might, without proper encouragement, undo all that had previously been taught.

Consequently, it is not surprising to find that the

Christian groups carried their control to the dramatic point when the witness must confess or deny. Doubtless their practice was learned from bitter experience, for it was early learned that defection had evil influence upon those yet to be examined.

In the first place, Christians who were being examined found that they were not left alone. It was usual for a number of their fellows to be present during the legal process. Naturally this was a factor of importance in the determination of the suspect's conduct. Doubtless it lent encouragement for him to be conscious that friends were present. Of still greater force was the perception that the candidate's own standing was importantly affected by their judgment of his conduct; presently he would be a hero to be praised or an apostate to be reviled. It has been shown that the approval or disapproval of one group or the other would control. The church group took care to exercise all possible influence to impress the candidate that eternal destiny weighted the scale of values in favor of confession, and saw to it that the witness would feel its influence at the critical time. Too, the fact that the general public saw the outcome was of great effect. Not infrequently a denier was greeted by the jeers of the bystanders.

The several elements of the control of suspects during the legal processes are determinable. There may be mentioned the effect of the publicity of the occasion. This may be seen in the mob action against Christians in Lyons and Vienne, which, as one of the earlier cases, occurred before the technique of control had been brought to its highest efficiency. In such a case it is not surprising that there was less unanimity in the conduct of the Christians, with the result that their behavior lacked the uniformity which later became so highly desired. As the famous Letter describes it,

The first went out rejoicing, glory and grace having blended in their faces, so that even their bonds seemed like beautiful ornaments. . . . . But the others were downcast and humble and dejected and filled with every kind of disgrace, and they were reproached by the heathen as ignoble and weak, bearing the accusation of murderers. . . . . The rest, beholding this, were strengthened, and when apprehended they confessed without hesitation [Eusebius *Church History* v. 1. 34 f.].

Then, it is alleged, when some who had denied saw the example of those who had confessed, they were influenced to alter their testimony and confess also: "The witnesses showed favor to those who had failed to witness . . . . for through their influence many who had denied were restored, and re-begotten, and rekindled with life, and learned to confess" (*ibid.*).

In the same incident the public spectacle of a notable martyrdom had tremendous effect; the woman Blandina was treated with unusual shamefulness, but the degree of severity is alleged to have had correspondingly powerful influence:

And because she appeared as if hanging upon a cross, and because of her earnest prayers, she inspired the combatants with great zeal. For they looked on her in her conflict, and beheld with their outward eyes in the form of their sister him who was crucified for them, that he might persuade those who believe on him that everyone who suffers for the glory of Christ has fellowship with the living God [*ibid*. v. 1. 41].

The publicity of the event is stressed by Tertullian as an argument for undertaking martyrdom: "The opportunity is given you when you are before the eyes of men. . . . . Seek to die the martyr's death, that he may be glorified who has suffered for you" (*Of Flight in Persecution* 9).

Secondly, the influence of the facial expression and gesture of the Christian bystanders had important effect. Eusebius calls attention to this factor; as a certain person who was being tried as a Christian appeared to be inclined to obey his judge and deny, a group of Christians who, not having yet been accused, were standing by

gnashed their teeth and made signs with their faces and stretched out their hands, and gestured with their bodies. And when the attention of all was turned to them, before anyone could seize them they rushed up to the tribunal saying that they were Christians, so that the governor and his council were affrighted. And those who were on trial appeared most courageous in prospect of their suffering, while their judges trembled. And they went exultingly from the tribunal rejoicing in their testimony, God himself having caused them to triumph gloriously [*Church History* vi. 41. 22 f.].

Cyprian is a witness to the power of leadership in influencing confession, as he writes,

And that nothing should be wanting to the example of good deeds in you, even now in the confession of your voice and the

suffering of your body you provoke the minds of your brethren to divine martyrdom, by exhibiting yourselves leaders of
virtue, that while the flock follows its pastors and imitates
what it sees to be done by those set over it, it may be crowned
with the like merits of obedience by the Lord [*Epistle*
lxxvi. 1].

Again, he cites the potent influence of concrete
example: "A manifold portion of the people, following your example, have confessed alike with
you" (*ibid.* lxxvi. 6).

An interesting example of the effectiveness of the
influence of the group upon wavering candidates is
found in a letter of the Roman congregation to
Cyprian in Carthage. Apparently a number of
Christians had concluded to make the sacrifice
which constituted the state's test of guilt, but their
fellows labored with them until the last moment,
for, as the letter reports, "we actually called back
some who were even mounting to the Capitol to
obey the summons to sacrifice" (*ibid.* viii).

Another aspect of the influence of the group is apparent in the lesson learned by the Christian leaders
that successful examples of martyrdom were salu-
tary only when accomplished in the martyr's home
surroundings. It was found that when death occurred elsewhere, the loss of effect upon the candidate and upon other Christians was serious. Consequently the wisdom of Cyprian appears as he
writes that "it is fit for a bishop in that city in
which he presides over the church of the Lord there
to confess the Lord, and that the whole people

should be glorified by the confession of their prelate in their presence" (*ibid*. lxxxii. 1). It had become a serious problem in his administration that banishment might precede the actual martyrdom, with the result that the profit of the martyr's example was lost. However, in one interesting case which arose, the sagacious leader makes an advantageous interpretation. A group of confessors who had been banished were returned to their home surroundings, which led Cyprian to write to them:

I and my colleagues . . . . entreat that he who is perfect and makes perfect will keep and perfect in you the glorious crown of your confession, who perchance has called you back for this purpose, that your glory should not be hidden, if the martyrdom of your confession should be consummated away from home. For the victim which affords an example to the brotherhood, both of courage and faith, ought to be offered up when the brethren are present [*ibid*. lvii. 4].

It is with exaggerating rhetoric, of course, that the treatise, *In Praise of Martyrdom*, mistakenly attributed to Cyprian, presents its exhortation. Nevertheless, its data in the present connection are not altogether irrelevant. For example, note the stress upon the publicity of the event:

Let it present itself to your eyes what a day that is when, with the people looking on, and all men watching, an undismayed devotion is struggling against earthly crosses and the threats of the world; how the minds in suspense, and hearts anxious about the tremblings of doubt, are agitated by the dread of the timid fearfulness of those who are congratulating them [*ibid*. 25].

Certain cases of the effect of public observation are cited by Eusebius:

We beheld the most wonderful ardor, and the truly divine energy and zeal of those who believed in the Christ of God. For as sentence was pronounced against the first, one after another rushed to the judgment seat and confessed themselves Christians [*Church History* viii. 9. 5].

A source reflecting the late and especially severe persecution activity makes the point of the power of group influence:

When the people see that men are lacerated by various kinds of tortures, and that they retain their patience unsubdued while their executioners are wearied, they think, as is really the case, that neither the agreement of so many nor the constancy of the dying is without meaning [Lactantius *Divine Institutes* v. 13].

But the group influence controlling the witness was not alone that of those fellow-Christians who were actually present with him or awaiting him in his familiar surroundings. Fully as powerful in control were the groups whose fellowship was in the realm of the imagination. The martyr was frequently controlled by so intangible a value as this type of imagery. Fellowship with God was a factor. It was made more definite by the thought of fellowship with Christ, especially in view of the fact that Christ was the great proto-martyr. Fellowship with other martyrs who had preceded him in suffering furnished comfort. Altogether the force of such imagined relations possessed influence quite comparable to that of one's immediate friends. The fact was turned to account by the Christian leaders in developing their processes of control in persecution.

It is this realm of association which occasions a typical figure by which the experience of martyrdom was pictured. The Graeco-Roman milieu had made familiar the stadium with its athletic contest. Tertullian took advantage of the institution to suggest the likeness of martyrdom, and in his simile significantly assigns important rôles to otherworldly beings and previously crowned martyrs:

You are about to pass through a noble struggle, in which the holy spirit is your trainer, in which the prize is an eternal crown of angelic essence. . . . . Therefore your master Jesus Christ . . . . has anointed you with his spirit, and led you into the arena [*Scorpiace* 3].

Cyprian uses another, the military figure. Persecution is a warfare, in which God, the angels, and Christ look down (*Epistle* lv. 8). Even more persuasively he writes,

Who would not bravely and unfalteringly receive a death precious in the sight of the Lord, to please his eyes who, looking down from above upon us who are placed in the conflict for his name, approves the willing, assists the struggling, crowns the conquering, with the recompense of patience, goodness, and affection [*ibid*. lvi. 4].

Moreover, it was not only impressed upon the martyr that these heavenly beings looked upon him but that Christ actually attended the martyr and aided him to bear his suffering. This view was current as early as the story of Polycarp's martyrdom, which explains the constancy of the martyrs by supposing that "the Lord was standing by and talking with them" (*Martyrdom of Polycarp* ii. 2). Such spiritism was quite in accord with Tertullian's thought, as may be seen as he writes, "They who have received him will never stoop to flee from persecution, nor to buy it off, for they have the Lord himself, one who will stand by us to aid us in suffering, as well as be our mouth when we are put to question" (*Of Flight in Persecution* 14). Again, he assures confessors that "the holy spirit has entered the prison with you" (*To the Martyrs* 1).

Skilful leader as Cyprian was, he made full use of the conception:

If the battle call you out, if the day of your contest shall come, engage bravely, fight with constancy, as knowing that you are fighting under the eyes of a present Lord, that you are attaining by the confession of his name to his own glory who is not such an one as that he only looks at his servants, but himself also wrestles in us, himself is engaged, himself in the struggles of our conflict not only crowns but is crowned [*Epistle* viii].

Or, to the same effect, "The frame wearied with labors lies prostrate on the ground, but it is no penalty to lie down with Christ" (*ibid.* lxxvi. 1).

It is in similar vein that Origen writes, "As we behold the martyrs coming from every church to be brought before the tribunal, we see in each the Lord himself condemned" (*Homily in Jeremiah* xiv. 7).

In this matter, as in others, the development of a concept which was current at an early date was much more luxuriant in the later literature. Much was made in the fully matured sources of the idea that Christ shared the martyr's suffering.[1] But in the present study attention is paid merely to the sources which reflect the earlier situations. Citations consequently are not made.

Other members of the fellowship which was suggested by mental representation were famous martyrs of the past. It ultimately became an interest in the church to show that practically every one of its founders suffered the martyr's death, and at a certain point in the development of this conception one finds it used as an element in the encouragement of candidates for martyrdom. Paul and Peter were the most famous of the exemplary line, and they were appealed to as such in as early a source as the letter of Clement of Rome (1 *Clement* 5–7). Clement of Alexandria thus refers to Matthew, Philip, Thomas, Levi, and many others (*Miscellanies* iv. 9). Polycarp's constancy won him the title of "apostolic . . . . teacher" (*Martyrdom of Polycarp* xvi. 2). According to Eusebius, Hegesippus makes a similar citation (*Church History* iii. 42. 8).

It was thus most fortunate for the persecuted Christian that he need not feel himself to be alone in the moment of his crisis. Experience in other similar cases proves that resolution flags lowest when the sense of loneliness is the strongest. But the candidate for martyrdom had a large roster of

---

[1] For example, cf. *Acts of John* 103; *Passion of S. Theodoret* 3; *Passion of S. Montanus* 21.

fellows. Standing by were some of the associates of his church group. The officials who were his ecclesiastical superiors were aware of his status. And, as his imagination lent itself to flights of comforting fancy, there were the whole line of heroes who before him, through suffering, had been victorious. Scripture taught him of many famed ones, and the rapidly growing Christian tradition was constantly adding to their number. He was persuaded that, if his courage did not fail, he was ever drawing nearer the apostles. Most dazzling in the whole prospect was the thought that God and Christ were supremely careful of his fate—more so, indeed, than were his earthly friends. Truly, beside the circle of present associates there was indeed a "crowd of heavenly witnesses."

Great as was the force of the influence of the group before and during the martyr's examination, it is of the utmost significance that it was not allowed to end as that crucial moment passed. It was found to be of the highest importance that fully as potent influence was exerted after the legal process was concluded. If the candidate had denied, effort was made to induce him to change his mind and alter his testimony. On the other hand, if he had affirmed his faith and accepted condemnation, the influence of the group was useful after the confession had been made. Attention followed the martyrs-designate while they were languishing in prison. It was a comforting assurance to the confessor that he would enjoy many favors while he possessed that rank. Charity operated in his behalf, so that his physical wants were not neglected. Of even greater importance was the prestige which he enjoyed as a confessor and a prospective martyr. But the matter did not end here; the candidate for martyrdom was assured of still more favorable position after his death. These were considerations which had tremendous influence over candidates.

The organization by which the churches cared for imprisoned confessors was highly efficient. It is possible to show that it was in operation at an early date, for in as early a work as the *Apology* of Aristides one reads, "And if they (Christians) hear that one of their number is imprisoned or afflicted on account of the name of their Messiah, all of them anxiously minister to his necessity, and if it is possible to redeem him they set him free" (*ibid.* 15). Justin speaks of the collection of funds "for those who are in bonds" (*Apology* 57). Tertullian notes and praises the custom: "These gifts . . . . are for . . . . [certain benevolent purposes are cited]. If there happen to be any in the mines, or banished to the islands, or shut up in the prisons, for nothing but their fidelity to the cause of God's church, they become the nurselings of their confessions" (*To the Martyrs* 1). Such collections are mentioned by Cyprian—for example, one gift of one hundred thousand sesterces (*Epistle* lix. 3; iv. 1). One source marks the receipt of such a gift (*ibid.* lxxix).

Again, the recognition of this custom by non-Christians is significant. Lucian ridiculed it, but in doing so became a witness to its widespread use. In his story of Proteus Peregrinus he tells how the charlatan took advantage of Christian benevolence:

However, now that he had been put in bonds, the Christians, looking upon the thing as a misfortune, left no stone unturned in their efforts to secure his release. Then when this proved to be impracticable, they all the time zealously rendered to him ministries of every other sort. . . . . They were wont to bring in all manner of viands and read their sacred Scriptures. . . . . Moreover, there came certain even from the cities of Asia, sent by the Christians from the common charge, to help the man, and advocate his cause, and comfort him. They exhibit extraordinary activity whenever some such thing occurs affecting their common interest. In short, they are lavish in everything. And what is more, on the pretext of his imprisonment, many contributions of money came to Peregrinus at that time, and he made no little income out of it [Of the Death of Peregrinus 11–13].

Undoubtedly, the practice of organized benevolence in the interest of prospective martyrs was an important element of control in persecution. For it must be kept in mind that many confessors, after a period in prison, were released. The assurance of care during imprisonment, together with the immense prestige enjoyed by virtue of being a confessor, possessed considerable attraction, especially in view of the possibility that release might follow imprisonment, with the consequent continuance of the prestige gained by confession.

But if the control of the witness before and during the legal examination, and the following of this by attention during imprisonment, were features of a process which commands the admiration, the fact that the social attitude of prestige was projected into the area of the life after the martyr's death is nothing short of amazing. This was effected through the cult of the martyr. One needs but to know something of the immense development of hagiography to perceive the far-reaching influence of this conception.

It became a part of the process of control in persecution to assure those who were liable to martyrdom that after their death they would be made the central figures of cults of veneration which verged upon worship. This assurance appears to have done much to make numbers of candidates the more willing to undergo an otherwise calamitous fate.

Just why the prospect of becoming the center of a cult should assist in building up the attitude of willingness to undertake martyrdom is less easy for the modern than for the ancient to see. But it must be remembered that the early Christians shared the pre-scientific world-view. It may not be amiss to point out that the similarity of the cult of the martyr to the familiar Graeco-Roman hero cults is not without significance.[1] The older conceptions of heroic behavior resulting in apotheosis doubtless paved the way for the rise and ready popularity of the martyr cult of the Christians, who naturally

[1] Cf. Lucius, *Die Anfänge des Heiligenkults in der Christlichen Kirche* (Tübingen, 1904); and Farnell, *Greek Hero Cults and the Idea of Immortality* (Oxford, 1921).

shared common conceptions of the same milieu. However, the modern set of attitudes is not without parallel. Perhaps the counterpart in the contemporary world is the zeal which induces persons to inoculate themselves with virulent bacteria, or to practice self-anesthesia, or to impair vital processes by experiments with short-wave electrical phenomena. Too, it is not long since there was an altogether common abandon of self-sacrifice in the cause of patriotism, which carried with it a similar veneration of soldier dead. There is no question that such a form of the social influence of prestige is immensely powerful in calling into play certain types of behavior.

At any rate, by the middle of the second century the cult of the martyr had reached a high stage of development. The main features may be simply stated. If possible, when a martyrdom was consummated, some part of the martyr's body was secured —a bone, a lock of hair, some drops of blood. If these might not be obtained, a remnant of the martyr's clothing, or something which he had used, served the purpose. What was salvable was regarded as a relic, and magical potency became attached to it. At certain intervals, chiefly upon the anniversary of the martyrdom, the relics were exhibited; and with these as cult objects some form of common religious service was held. The veneration accorded his memory and visibly organized about his relics cannot have been of less than profound influence upon the prospective martyr. He assumed a position of even cosmic significance, since as an intermediate object of devotion and an intercessor he was commonly supposed importantly to influence the eternal fate of those left behind. The relation of the story of his heroism as a part of the cult service insured the maintenance of his heroic reputation. Heroism in life not seldom verges upon worship, but to persons of a certain mental disposition to become the center of a religious cult is the achievement of a goal which is high indeed.

These features of the cult of the martyr may be seen as early as the writing of the first of the typical martyrologies, *The Martyrdom of Polycarp*. This source states,

We took up his [Polycarp's] bones, more precious than precious stones and finer than gold, and put them where it is meet. There the Lord will permit us to come together according to our power in gladness and joy, and celebrate the birthday of his martyrdom [*ibid*. xviii. 2].

The control purpose of the martyr cult is for the present study the central theme; it is of the highest importance to find it thus early explicitly stated: ". . . . both in memory of those who have already contested, and for the practice and training of those whose fate it shall be" (*ibid*. xviii. 3). One may well be surprised to observe the cult of the martyr so early mentioned, as though it were already fully developed. It must be supposed that back of such a reference as this lie the earlier stages of growth. If so, the early flourishing of the martyr cult is a striking phenomenon, useful as it undoubtedly was in control in persecution.

Tertullian notes that "as often as the anniversary comes round, we make offering for the dead as birthday honors" (*Of the Crown* 3). Cyprian also takes account of the custom: "We always offer sacrifices for them, as you remember, as often as we celebrate the passions and days of the martyrs in annual commemoration" (*Epistle* xxxiii. 3). Again, he instructs his flock to "take note of their days on which they depart, that we may celebrate their commemoration among the memorials of the martyrs" (*ibid.* xxxvi. 2). Further, to the same effect, "There are celebrated here by us oblations and sacrifices for their commemorations, which things, with the Lord's protection, we shall soon celebrate with you" (*ibid.*).

No notice is taken in the present connection of the luxuriant growth of the cult of the martyr in the later stages, when the church made such use of the institution that the hagiographers have not even yet completed the compilation of the literature of the acts of the martyrs.[1] It may be mentioned, however, that the process of assigning dates for notable martyrdoms, compiling conventional stories of their deaths, and synchronizing their traditional anniversaries with the liturgy, goes well back into the imperial period. But even in limiting attention to the earlier periods the significance of the cult as a

---

[1] Cf., for example, the volumes published by the Bollandist Society.

factor in inducing the attitude of willingness to undergo the fate of martyrdom is apparent.

The use of relics in the cult of the martyr is also witnessed by contemporaries. The collection of relics of the body of Polycarp will be remembered from the citations above. Other examples may be offered. For example, the chronicler of the life and passion of Cyprian notes that a certain Thesserarius offered to exchange clothing with the prospective martyr, being motivated, the writer says, by the desire to possess a relic which he confidently expected would become famous: "He doubtless coveted nothing further in respect of his proffered kindness than to possess the now blood-stained sweat of the martyr going to God" (*Life and Passion of Cyprian* 16).

The eagerness to possess such relics was another custom of the Christians which was satirized by Lucian in his story of Peregrinus. He pictures the people, after the self-immolation of the dubious hero, as hurrying to secure some memento. The terminology itself is significant; the satirist uses the term λείψανον (*Of the Death of Peregrinus* 13), which was also used by Gregory Nazianzen in his work, *On the Martyrs*.

The special position of martyrs as intercessors for those remaining behind has already been noted as one of the sanctions of reward. It may further be mentioned in the present connection. Cyprian's statement suggests that the belief in the intercessory office of the martyr was thoroughly popular:

We believe, indeed, that the merits of the martyrs and the works of the righteous are of great avail with the Judge, but that will be when the day of judgment shall come, when, after the conclusion of this life and the world, his people shall stand before the tribunal of Christ [*Treatise* iii. 17].

The report of Eusebius of a request made to a group of Palestinian martyrs is to the same effect: a woman asked that they would "remember her when they came before the Lord" (*Martyrs of Palestine* vii. 1). The consciousness on the part of future martyrs that they should presently occupy an intercessory position of no less than cosmic implication was doubtless of considerable effect in sustaining their ideal of dying for their faith.

It is thus possible to exhibit the details of the manner in which the influence of the Christian groups secured its effect upon those members who were liable to examination by the officials of the state. It is of great interest that in general (and in certain particulars) the societies exercised forces of social control in exactly the manner which has been found by modern social science to be necessary to secure like results. Doubtless the technique was acquired by trial and error and applied with a certain amount of *naïveté;* but however this may be, the process of control by which the early Christian groups maintained their integrity in the face of persecution is an interesting, as well as an important, example of social influence.

Obviously, the process succeeded because, consciously or unconsciously applied, it was correctly organized and soundly based. It is not to be thought that martyrs in any significant number could have undergone their fate if they had been abandoned in it by their fellow-Christians. They were able to meet their crisis only because they were members of societies which kept effective the influence of their social bonds. That such influence was operative before and during the time of confession, and even after the confession had been secured, while the confessor lay in prison, or actually, as he fondly supposed, after his faithfulness unto death, accounts for the maintenance of the martyr's courage. In other words, he was enabled to emerge through the painful course of punishment because he was one of a number. He was such a person as he proved to be because of group influences, of which, for this purpose, his Christian fellowship was the most effective. It was because of his integration as one of a group that he was thus controllable. The essential factor in control was the influence, variously applied, of the group.

V

THE METHOD OF CONTROL

The technique of the control of the persecuted may readily be discovered by the analysis of the literature in which the experiences of, and the exhortations to, the martyrs are recounted. It consisted of the generation in the prospective martyr of the wish that such constancy might be maintained when subject to legal examination that the suspected or accused Christian would confess rather than deny his membership in a Christian society. The wish was reinforced by vividly urged sanctions of reward for success and punishment for failure. The effect of the association of fellow-Christians in church assembly, in ritual, in Scripture-reading, and in common worship was strong. Probably in the majority of cases of martyrdom there was a psychic basis which might fairly be called abnormal; such a basis made the effect of preparation and association the greater. The approval or disapproval of fellow-Christians was balanced, and in many cases with greater weight, against the approval or disapproval of fellow-subjects whose cult affiliations were satisfactory to the state. Exhortations of those in authority, especially of confessors; the example of other martyrs; and the prominence accruing from the experience—all operated powerfully to induce the attitude of willingness to under-

take confession and perhaps martyrdom. The magical effect of martyrdom and the unparalleled prestige of the martyr as an object of veneration were
often effectual inducements.

Such were the elements of the technique of control. What were the methods of applying the technique which was learned from experience? As it has
been urged, the element of simplicity in the situation which made the task of the Christian leaders
not an impossible one was the purely dichotomous
aspect of the dilemma. The suspected or accused
Christian had either to confess or to deny his guilt
(unless, indeed, he resorted to bribery, simulation,
or some other form of evasion). Since the alternative which faced the prospective confessor had the
advantage of simplicity, the effort of those attempting to control the witness might be directed to a
specific and well-known end. This factor appears to
have brought into play quite definite methods of
control.

From what have been exhibited as elements in
the technique of control, certain aspects of method
were directly applied upon the Christian who was
liable. Previous to the appearance of any such in
court the Christians in common assemblies had
been to some extent prepared for what was to occur. Common worship, prayers for strength, the
celebration of a noble death in ritualistic drama,
the hearing of Scripture readings or of exhortations, all secured result as face-to-face contact operated in control. In certain cases assembly for the

reading of communications brought to the face-to-face group the heartening stimulus of the experiences of fellows who had been removed from physical presence. It cannot be too strongly urged that fellowship in common meeting is one of the most efficient of all social forces.

Further, as has been pointed out, the progress of the witness to the court was attended by face-to-face contact with his fellows. Even during the conduct of the legal examination such contact was maintained by at least a few of the suspect's fellow-Christians. And, as has already been suggested, his associates found ways by means of which access might be had to those who had met the situation successfully and were in prison, awaiting the day when the next step in their heroic progress was to be undertaken. Not only thus far, but the very torture and death of martyrs were in many cases observed by certain of their co-religionists. To such length extended the physical contact of their associates with the martyrs.

In all such relationships the face-to-face contact of fellow-Christians was utilized as method by which various elements of the technique of control were applied. The social influence of common worship has already been described. Such methods as those of assembly are obvious enough to require no further discussion. Less obvious, but certainly more dramatic, is the force of direct method during the course of the examination. Cases in which gesture, facial expression, and the like, by which certain wavering witnesses were made to confess when they were at the very point of denying, are highly instructive. Examples in which confessions were secured although denial had already been made, when apostates were shamed into confession by the voluntary surrender and persuasive behavior of bystanders, are equally significant. The well-known cases of the dissuasion of disheartened Christians when on their way to sacrifice are eloquent of the effect of face to face contact.

The effect of direct contact was of course enhanced by attending factors. Consider, for example, the strengthening of the already powerful influence of common worship by the dramatic values of ritual, which by the third century was rapidly advancing in color and splendor. Add to the bond of unity the emotional influence of song, to the effect of biblical examples of martyrdom the institutional value which was carried by the sacredness ascribed to Scripture. As an example of personal relationship, the authority of officials was constantly increasing: the bishop, always more than a mere person, always himself something of the nature of an institution, was steadily becoming more powerful. It is quite clear, even though the prestige of some bishops was impaired by flight or "retirement," that their authority was not inconsiderable, while, proportionately, the influence of a group of bishops in conclave was still more awful. The face-to-face intercourse with an imprisoned confessor was always regarded as a privilege; obviously the importance of such contact was tremendously increased by the fact that he was not merely a prospective, but an actual confessor and daily the more nearly approaching his martyrdom.

It needs not to be labored that the influence of what the sociologist calls the "primary group," the group in face-to-face contact, was strong. It may be concluded, as has indeed been shown by the citation of illustrations of the technique of control, that those methods which may be designated as "immediate" were of the highest importance.

But it is extremely interesting that Christian leadership utilized methods of control which were of another sort. Methods which did not depend upon face-to-face contact, but which were therefore secondary or mediate, were utilized. Effective as was the personal appearance of the bishop, the force of the physical presence of a fellow-confessor, or the helpful visit of one's associates, these direct contacts were not always possible. Upon certain occasions some of the bishops "retired" for a season. The funds which secured access to, and comfort of, imprisoned confessors were not unlimited. It is not difficult to imagine that witnesses not seldom felt that they were alone, unless, as was frequently the case, they were persuaded that their heavenly advocates were with them. In such situations mediated methods must be employed.

It has already been suggested that certain martyrs endured their fate with ordinary sensibilities quite inhibited by the imagery of the presence of spirit companions. A part of the technique of control was the impartation of the conviction that Jesus was a fellow-sufferer and that God and the heroes of other days were a cloud of heavenly martyrs. This aspect of the martyr attitude is one element of the mediated methods of control.

But it would naturally be supposed, without unduly discounting the effect of otherworldly imagination, that the ultimate trust would not rest upon so intangible a method. The leaders of the Christian churches were not altogether devoid of the wisdom of this age. In the absence of direct physical contact, indirect means of keeping in touch with their flocks, and particularly those nearest to the surveillance of the state, were found, so that control, though by mediated methods, was nevertheless maintained.

The same substitute for physical contact which resulted in the epistolary collection represented by Paul's letters in the New Testament occurred to the retired bishops. The letters of Cyprian have in the present study been abundantly quoted; evidently he, as a skilful leader, found the letter to be very useful. He might write when and where he was unable to visit. Of course, Cyprian was not the only one to use the letter for such purpose. The use of the letter form was extensive, as will be recalled from the distribution of the epistolary sources which have been cited. Cyprian wrote to churches, and churches responded to Cyprian; he wrote to confessors, and they to him. Bishops wrote in groups to their flocks. Origen addressed a fervid letter to his father. Confessors wrote certificates of peace to penitent apostates. The Christians of Lyons and Vienne wrote the famous letter so fortunately quoted by Eusebius, describing the calamities which had befallen them and chronicling the heroic behavior of some of their number. The story of Polycarp's martyrdom is in letter form. Ignatius' letters may be mentioned in the present connection, so ardently do they breathe the desire of the bishop to become a martyr. As shall be suggested later, the interest in control in situations approaching the nature of persecution appears in several letters which were written close to the time of the writing of parts of the New Testament, and, indeed, in letters forming parts of the New Testament itself. The collection of groups of these letters is a highly interesting phenomenon.[1]

Another element in the use of writing as a mediate method of control in persecution is the abundant apologetic literature of the Christians. This type of writing began at a relatively early date, so that it is instructive of method during periods in which techniques of control were in process of evolution. The apologies were first directed to the defense of the Christian movement against Judaism;[2] but as Christians began to come to the attention of the state, those addressed to the emperors became

[1] Goodspeed, *New Solutions of New Testament Problems* (Chicago, 1928).

[2] Riddle, *Jesus and the Pharisees, A Study in Christian Tradition* (Chicago, 1928), pp. 145–66.

current.[1] But it may be surmised that to whomever
ostensibly they were addressed, the real public of
the political apologies was the Christian groups
themselves, and their true purpose the bolstering of
this public in the trying situations in which it found
itself.

It may be affirmed that the most useful part of
the apologies was their rehearsal of the arguments
by which the innocuousness of Christianity was
proven and the propriety of its free exercise was
established. The telltale features are those which
presumably were more relevant to the edification of
Christians than the information of the emperor.
Just as such a formal anti-Jewish apology as Justin's *Dialogue with Trypho* was replete with stock
arguments whose purpose was the knocking-down
of the straw man of the opposition, so the political
defenses, such as Justin's or Tertullian's, were useful in controlling adherents of Christian groups.
They were intended to reassure the fearful, encourage the timid, and furnish that sense of solidarity which is the prime essential of maintaining a group consciousness which has recently been
achieved but which is in danger of disintegration.

Clearly the circulation of the apologies and their
preservation were by the efforts of Christians. This
obviously implies their control purpose. For example, when it became in point for a Christian writer
to compile what passed for a history of the Chris-

[1] Bigelmair, *Die Beteiligung der Christen am öffentlichen Leben in vorconstantinischer Zeit* (München, 1902), pp. 82 ff.

tian movement,[1] the apologies were among those other writings of the church fathers which were available as sources.

The apologies reflect a social situation in which the Christians, having made an effort to come to terms with Roman society, but for certain reasons finding themselves objects of suspicion and opposition, found it necessary aggressively to assert their right to exist. But, as is well known, the intellectual assertion of a right to exist is infinitely less effective than the general impartation of the conviction to that effect among those who propose to continue their existence. The arguments of the apologies have exactly this pragmatic character.

Further, it is exactly such purpose which marks the difference in flavor between two such representative apologies as those of Justin and Tertullian. The impassioned ardor of the African's plea as over against the reasoned logic of the Asian's indicates not merely a difference in the personalities of their authors but also an advance in the situations which the works were intended to meet, together with a notable advance in the skill with which the technique of control found expression in an efficient method.

Still another type of writing is to be mentioned among the mediate methods of control. When martyrdom had become a status whose eminence was certified by public acclaim and cult veneration, its value was vehemently asserted in fervid exhorta-

[1] The *Church History* of Eusebius.

tions. The two best-known examples of this literature are Origen's *Exhortation to Martyrdom* and the
rhetorical *In Praise of Martyrdom*, which was, without warrant, attributed to Cyprian. To what extent these writings were influential in winning their
purpose is uncertain. Their extravagance lays them
open to suspicion. One wonders whether their authors represent any general point of view, or
whether they are not merely the articulation of so
extremely emotional a reaction that they actually
reflect a set of attitudes which must be characterized as abnormal. Certainly no one would doubt
that Origen's enthusiasm for the status of martyr
was eccentric, especially in view of the psychopathic elements of his personality which have been
pointed out. But even after as frank a discount of
the pragmatic character of these works as may
reasonably be made, the facts of their currency and
their preservation among other patristic writings
witness a certain amount of influence, whatever its
extent may have been. It is clear that the oral exhortations to martyrdom were highly effective; it
may be supposed that literary expression of the
same arguments was useful to some degree.

But of all the types of writing which were used to
exploit the technique of control in persecution, that
known as the "martyrology" was undoubtedly the
most influential. This form of literature early
reached typical organization, and enjoyed so con-
tinuous a currency that the volume of extant speci-

mens is enormous.[1] As a matter of fact, the materials are still in process of collection and publication. To be sure, for the present purpose no attention need be paid to the immense number of martyrologies which were composed after the period of the persecutions; these represent a cult interest which has slight connection with the subject of investigation, save as the hagiographical volume grew out of the cult of the martyr.

The martyrologies, as has been said, conform to a type. They were written ostensibly as reports of the confessor's examination and the martyr's death. Sometimes the story of the court proceedings is prefaced by the relation of events leading up to it, the rise of the action which led to the martyr's arrest, some account of his earlier life, and an account of his behavior immediately before the final events. But the essential features are those which describe the activity of the witness during and after the examination. Usually the dialogue between the judge and the witness is graphically reported in considerable detail. The martyr's fortitude, his bearing while he was being examined, and his dignity under abuse are all pictured with more or less verisimilitude. In the cases where his torture is described, the details are often unpleasant to modern taste. Not infrequently the ancient-world view is patently reflected in the description of supernatural portents which are alleged to have occurred.

[1] Harnack, *Geschichte der altchristlichen Litteratur* (Leipzig, 1904), II, 807.

The martyrologies appear to have reached their typical form by the middle of the second century. The *Martyrdom of Polycarp* is at once an early and the perfect example of the type. Other early examples which are almost equally representative are the *Acts of Justin* and the *Acts of the Scillitan Martyrs*. After these came a host of specimens. To the great bulk of these, since their rise was occasioned simply by the interest in adding to the number of saints on the church's calendar, no attention need be paid in the present study.

Nevertheless, the volume of the martyrologies which were produced during the period of the persecutions presents a problem which is relevant to this investigation of their use as instruments of social control. Even though scholarly analysis has thus reduced the number of the older martyrologies, it is apparent upon examination that the interest in the cult of the martyr has operated in the composition and the collection of these, so that further distinction must be made.

There are several representative classifications of the martyrological literature. The patrologist Bardenhewer[1] distinguishes the official documents (records, *acta*, *gesta*, made by the court notaries but circulated by the Christians), narratives based upon the testimony of eyewitnesses, and the much larger but less valuable mass belonging to the later periods, usually enlarging upon and ornamenting the

[1] *Patrology* (St. Louis, 1908), pp. 228 f.

authentic accounts. Niedermeyer[1] emphasizes the importance of date in distinguishing the authentic from the merely hagiographical; acts which bear no date or which are not to be dated with certainty are much less trustworthy than those whose dates may be determined or corroborated. Delehaye[2] divides the whole literature into six classes: official reports, reports of eyewitnesses, *acta* of which the principal sources are from one or other of these two classes, *acta* with no written source but with an actual event as the basis, imaginative romances, and forgeries. A recent classification is by the Italian scholar, Manaresi,[3] who finds separable groups as follows: works which reproduce the court report, reports of eyewitnesses, documents which essentially rewrite some such trustworthy report, traditional accounts, and deliberately romancing stories.

As may be seen from these analyses, the criterion of originality or authenticity is the nearness of approach to the reproduction of the court proceedings. It is this factor which leads other scholars—for example, Conybeare[4] and Thompson[5]—to emphasize the presence of dialogue as the essential element of a primitive martyrology.

On the basis of such principles of analysis, the

[1] *Über antike Protokoll-Litteratur* (Göttingen, 1918).

[2] *Legends of the Saints* (London, 1907), pp. 111–15.

[3] *L'impero romano e il Christianesimo* (Torino, 1914), pp. 22, 22–24.

[4] *The Apology and Acts of Apollonius* (London, 1894), pp. 14, 94 f.

[5] *American Journal of Theology*, XVI (1912), 359–84.

patrologists to whom reference has been made[1] have with general agreement identified certain martyrologies as authentic. The list of those which bear the stamp of approval include works which may be read in almost any representative collection of acts of martyrs[2]—for example: *The Martyrdom of Polycarp; The Acts of the Scillitan Martyrs; The Acts of Justin; The Letter of the Churches of Lyons and Vienne; The Passion of SS. Perpetua and Felicitas; The Acts of Pionius; The Acts of SS. Carpus, Paphylus, and Agathonice;* and a few others.

These representative documents formed certainly the most subtle and perhaps the most effective part of the mediate method of control. They were apparently written early, as the approximation of the legal verbiage would indicate. The official court records themselves, it is suggested, were purchased for the purpose of circulation in their rewritten form. To quote Doulcet: "The legal reports were written at the hearing by the pagan notaries, and then deposited in the archives. The Christians found means of obtaining copies which they reproduced in the religious style, or developed in different ways."[3] The historian Bigelmair calls attention to the same method of writing and cites the use made of the materials obtained from the archives by Eusebius

[1] E.g., Knopf, *Ausgewählte Märtyrerakten* (Tübingen, 1913).

[2] Cf. also Holl, "Die Vorstellung vom Märtyrer und die Märtyrerakten in Ihrer Geschichtlichen Entwickelung," *Neue Jahrbücher für das Klassische Altertum*, XXXIII (1914), 521–56; and Harnack, *op. cit.*, II, 216–20.

[3] Doulcet, *Essai sur les rapports de l'église chrétienne avec l'état romain* (Paris, 1882), p. 83 n.

and (later) by Jerome and Rufinus.[1] Workman reports the interesting datum of the purchase for two hundred denarii of the copy of the official report of the trial of Tarachus, Probus, and Andronicus in 304.[2]

It is possible to observe something of the circulation of these works. As a fortunate part of its contents the *Martyrdom of Polycarp* is of great value for this detail. Its control purpose appears in the Introduction:

We write to you, brethren, the story of the martyrs and of the blessed Polycarp . . . . for one might almost say that all that had gone before happened in order that the Lord might show to us from above a martyrdom in accordance with the Gospel [*ibid*. i].

Toward the conclusion of the work the wider circulation of the document is requested:

You, indeed, asked that the events might be explained to you at length, but we have for the present explained them in a summary by our brother Marcion; therefore when you have heard these things, send the letter to the brethren farther on, that they also may glorify the Lord, who takes his chosen ones from his own servants [*ibid*. xx. 1].

But in addition, there are several details of its further literary history:

Gaius copied this from the writing of Irenaeus, a disciple of Polycarp, and he lived with Irenaeus, and I, Socrates, wrote it out in Corinth, from the copies of Gaius. Grace be with you all. And I, again, Pionius, wrote it out from the former

[1] Bigelmair, *op cit.*, p. 141.

[2] Workman, *Persecution in the Early Church* (Cincinnati, 1906), p. 285.

writings, after searching for it, because the blessed Polycarp showed it to me in a vision [*ibid.* xxii. 2, 3].

To this, according to one manuscript authority, there is added:

This account Gaius copied from the writings of Irenaeus. . . . . From these papers of Irenaeus, then, as was stated above, Gaius made a copy, and Isocrates used in Corinth the copy of Gaius. And again I, Pionius, wrote from the copies of Isocrates, according to the revelation of the holy Polycarp, after searching for them, and gathering them together when they were worn out from age.[1]

Even earlier than this the letters of Ignatius, which had in them not a little of instructive reflection of the attitudes which controlled the martyrs, had wide circulation. Irenaeus quoted from the most ardent of the Ignatian letters in his discussion of persecution (*Against Heresies* v. 28. 4). Origen, who also was possessed of the most intense conviction of the value of martyrdom, cited "certain Epistles" of Ignatius in one of his homilies (*Homily in Luke* 6).

Later practice is to the same effect. The extensive use of writing by Cyprian has already been discussed. It may be added that he not only circulated writings of his own but caused the wider reading of other materials which were useful for his purpose. For example, he once wrote, "I have sent also copies of the letter which the strong and noble Celerinus wrote to Lucianus, and also Lucianus'

[1] Conclusion of the Moscow MS; cf. Lake, *The Apostolic Fathers*, II, 343 f.

answer" (*Epistle* xxvii. 3). On another occasion he wrote to the Carthaginian clergy:

We request that you who have a zeal for God to send a copy of this letter to whomsoever you are able, as occasions may serve, or make your own opportunities, or send a message, that they may stand firm and stedfast in the faith [*ibid*. ii. 3].

As a further point, the collection of the works on martyrdom and their use as associated materials establish the fact that their control purpose was uppermost. Eusebius, in compiling his *Church History*, was able to quote extensively from martyrologies and similar materials. He several times mentions a collection made by himself (*ibid*. iv. 15. 5; Prologue v. 4; v. 21), which unfortunately has been lost. There is preserved in his history a collection of the stories of the martyrs of Palestine, and extracts from another collection furnish what he reports of martyrdoms which occurred in Alexandria (*ibid*. vii. 10). The *Passion of SS. Perpetua and Felicitas* contains an interesting note, which clearly suggests the practical purpose of such compositions: "If ancient illustrations . . . . are collected in writing, so that by the perusal of them . . . . man may be strengthened, why should not new instances also be collected . . . . ?" (*ibid*. Prologue).

So far as content is concerned, the briefest examination of the martyrologies is sufficient to exhibit their control purpose. The form given them as the legal processes were rewritten at once stamps them,

in the words of Krüger,[1] as "stories with a purpose."
Essentially the same seems to be the judgment of
of Geffcken, when he notes that "most of the *acta*,
with the exception of the *Acts of the Scillitan Martyrs*, a genuine original document, are embellished
for the reader, for the edification of the faithful."[2]

These embellishments, which furnish the element
of purpose in the stories, may be noted even in
those martyrologies which are more nearly primitive. Those which preserve in greater part the form
of a report of the court dialogue contain language
which obviously would not have been included in a
state document. It is not impossible that the court
record might contain the argumentative data with
which the confessor lectured his judge, or perhaps
the lengthy Scripture quotations which not infrequently appear. But it is hardly likely that the
original document would contain, for example, the
doxology with which the report was usually closed.
As an example, that primitive document excepted
from the process of pragmatic embellishment by
Geffcken, the *Acts of the Scillitan Martyrs*, closes
with the words, "while our Lord Jesus Christ is
reigning, to whom be all glory, honor, and worship,
with all the saints and the living spirit now and to
the ages of ages, amen." The relatively unadorned
Acts of Justin carries the conclusion:

The holy martyrs having glorified God, and having gone
forth to the accustomed place, were beheaded, and perfected

[1] "Literature on Church History," *Harvard Theological Review*, XIV
(1921), 302.

[2] Geffcken, *Aus der Werdezeit des Christentums* (Leipzig, 1909), p. 56.

their testimony in the confession of the Savior. And some of the faithful, having secretly removed their bodies, laid them in a suitable place, the grace of our Lord Jesus Christ having wrought along with them, to whom be glory forever, amen.

Other striking phenomena appear in the more primitive works. In the *Martyrdom of Polycarp* the most telling feature is the deliberate attempt to relate the story of the hero with subtle reference to parallels in the story of Jesus' martyrdom. This is what seems to be in the mind of the writer when he characterizes Polycarp's death as a martyrdom "in accordance with the Gospel." It is stated that the noble martyr waited to be betrayed "as also the Lord had done" (*ibid.* i. 2). They who betrayed him were of his own house (vi. 2). The police captain had "the very name, being called Herod" (*ibid.*). His betrayers shall suffer the same punishment as did Judas (*ibid.*). "Taking the slave the police and cavalry went out on Friday, with their usual arms, as though they were advancing against a robber" (vii. 1). They "set him on an ass and led him into the city on a great sabbath day" (viii. 1). He predicted his own death (v. 2). There was heard a voice from heaven to encourage the disciples (ix. 1). There were miracles attending his death (xv; xvi. 1). Very probably the references to the "great sabbath" are in conscious imitation of the references in the Fourth Gospel (John 19:31), where the same words are used.[1]

Further, the attempt was made to link Polycarp

[1] Riddle, "A Literary Allusion in the Martyrdom of Polycarp," *Anglican Theological Review*, VIII (1925), 136–42.

with the line of the apostles. It was claimed that he was an apostolic and a prophetic teacher (*Martyr-dom of Polycarp* xvi. 2). The interest in ascribing prophetic inspiration to martyrs appears frequently in the later martyrologies. In this case the charism of prophecy is bestowed; interestingly enough, the martyr Ignatius in his letter to Polycarp had urged him to strive for it (*ibid.*), and the story of the martyrdom assures its readers that the goal had been attained.

These and other similar details figure in other martyrologies in the same useful manner. The parallels to the passion of Jesus early became one of the vital interests in the whole literature on martyrdom. Ignatius on the way to a death in the Roman arena prayed that he might follow the passion of his Lord (Ignatius *To the Romans* vi. 3). The Lyons and Vienne letter characterizes martyrdom as the imitation of Christ (Eusebius *Church History* v. 2. 3) and refers to the details of Blandina's death as a specific instance (*ibid.* v. 1. 41). Irenaeus notes that those who die for their confession are such as those "who strive to follow the footsteps of the Lord's passion" (*Against Heresies* iii. 18. 5). Clement of Alexandria makes the same point of imitation (*Miscellanies* iii. 9). Cyprian was sufficiently struck by the coincidence that he spoke of the club with which confessors were beaten and the wood of Jesus' cross (*Epistle* lxxvi. 2), and often makes the specific suggestion that martyrdom was the imitation of Christ (*ibid.* xxv; xxxvi. 1; lxxvi. 7). Perpetua's flagellation was regarded as "a part of that which was suffered by Christ" (*Passion of SS. Perpetua and Felicitas* 18). A certain Nemesion, "like Christ, was executed with criminals" (Eusebius *Church History* vi. 41); while in another case, "With Agapus was delivered another Barabbas" (Eusebius *Martyrs of Palestine* vi); and the freeing of a criminal while a confessor was executed was said to have been "almost like Barabbas in the time of our Savior" (*ibid.* vi. 5).

As has been pointed out, much was made of the posture of death in the form of the cross; the examples of Blandina in the Lyons and Vienne group and of the Palestinian martyr mentioned by Eusebius have already been cited. A further point of imitation was made in the case of the martyrs Montanus and Lucius, from whose sides, as in the instance related of Jesus, it was alleged that blood and water issued (*Passion of SS. Montanus and Lucius* 22). In the later literature one finds Lactantius' direct reference to the death of Jesus as a pattern (*Divine Institutes* iv. 26) and Augustine's comparison of Cyprian with Christ (*Sermon* 209).

Similar to the interest in relating the experiences of the martyrs with conscious parallelism to the story of Jesus is the attempt also to suggest similarity to the experiences of the apostles. This is reflected in the martyrological writing of Clement of Alexandria, Tertullian, and still more abundantly in the later literature. The full fruit of this interest was, of course, the composition of that literature in which a romantic history, in almost every case including a martyrdom, is furnished each of the faithful twelve, beside those others who, although not of this fellowship, yet were called apostles.

These effective details were characteristically introduced by a particularized convention in writing.[1] The martyr is pictured always as master of the situation in which he is placed. He is not convicted by his judge, but by his wise answers his judge is refuted. He is never carried to an unwelcome fate by untoward circumstance, but always is pictured as laying down his life of himself. The confessor is always successful in his defense, even though he must needs be given a sentence of condemnation. The martyr is always the fully delineated hero.

In view of the operation of these pragmatic interests it is not surprising that in style the martyrology is related to the Greek literary apologia. Geffcken, pointing out the influences of the Maccabean books upon the Lyons and Vienne letter, aptly notices the formal relation in the manner in which the wretched sufferers speak in apologetic apopthegmata. Other examples, such as the stories of Carpus, of the Scillitan martyrs, of Pionius, of Procopius, and others, exhibit such influence. The *Acts of St. Achatus* are highly argumentative, and the story of the martyrdom of Apollonius abounds in data which bear relation with the philosophical writings.

It is an irresistible conclusion that the voluminous literature of martyrdom was a part of the

[1] Delehaye, *op. cit.*, pp. 24 f.

method by which the technique of control was applied. The several types of this literature, and most particularly the martyrologies, were designed chiefly to present in an exemplary and illustrative manner the arguments for the acceptance of martyrdom. They were written in part to inform, but much more importantly to edify. Their most essential purpose was to suggest, with appropriate sanctions, that the experience of the martyr was one which it was desirable to imitate. To generate this wish, and to multiply this attitude, the martyrologies were written and assiduously circulated. Their content was subtly presented, so that the reader through the heroic history of famed saints was equipped with an answer for every question, and, more effective than this, was taught that the fate of the hero was so richly glorified that the reading of such stories not seldom was found to be sufficiently impelling that their readers themselves joined the noble army of martyrs.

It may not be amiss to conclude a discussion of the method of control by offering certain statements in concrete evidence of the efficiency of the mediate method. It has been found advisable always to regard the more enthusiastic and emotional of the literature of martyrdom with reserve. Doubtless such caution is a proper attitude in scientific research. Nevertheless, it is interesting to read a contemporary witness to the effectiveness of representative exhortation. A letter to Cyprian, who had interested himself on behalf of confessors, reads as follows:

We ought to give you . . . . and do give you abundant thanks, that you have brightened the darkness of their prison by your letters, that you came to them by whatever way you could enter, that you refreshed their minds, robust in their own faith and confession, by your addresses and letters, that, following up their felicities with worthy praises you have inflamed them to a much more ardent desire for heavenly glory, that you urged them forward, that you animated by the power of your discourse those who, as we believe and hope, will be victors by and by, so that although all may seem to come from the faith of those who confess and from divine mercy, yet they seem in their martyrdom to have become in some sort debtors to you [Cyprian *Epistle* xxx. 5].

An example of the similar effect of the martyrology is furnished in the familiar *Passion of SS. Perpetua and Felicitas*, whose Prologue aptly states the propriety of offering contemporary as well as ancient examples of heroic behavior. After the martyrdoms of its story are described, the work closes with another statement of its hope:

O most brave and blessed martyrs! O truly called and chosen unto the glory of our Lord Jesus Christ! whom whoever magnifies and honors and adores assuredly ought to read these examples for the edification of the church not less than the ancient ones, so that new virtues also may testify that one and the same holy spirit is always operating even now [*ibid*. vi. 4].

There can be no doubt that the immediate influence of the group upon its single adherents, known to be powerful, was matched by the skilful and effective influence mediated through the several conventional sorts of writing.

VI

THE BASIS OF CONTROL

Both the immediate influence of face-to-face contact and the mediate influence of literary composition formed the method of the control of the prospective martyrs. Apparently these several aspects of method were measurably successful, since, besides the host of gratuitously canonized martyrs of tradition, there were those, in no small number, whose fate is well attested; and, as is obvious, the church emerged the victor in its contest with the state.

There was, of course, a basis of control which made success possible. Social control necessarily presupposes a psychological basis.[1] Individuals, so-called, are always to a degree subject to control by the influence of their associates. The degree of such control varies, but it is only in the rarest cases that the area of social control tends toward a meager limit. The production of personality itself is due to the influence of the group with which one is associated; and in the growth of personality it is of critical importance to what particular groups the individual by environment, choice, or chance is joined. The infant, for example, is inevitably one of a group. Biologically he is produced by the junction of two elements; and from birth he necessarily

[1] For example, cf. E. S. Bogardus, *Essentials of Social Psychology* (Los Angeles, 1923); *Fundamentals of Social Psychology* (New York, 1924).

belongs to social groups, if he survives. The family unit as primary is presently supplemented by play and school groups, and subsequently the range of such relations is increasingly wider. These contacts are of basic importance.

Religious groups are examples of such influence, differing in no essential particular from other group relationships.[1] A person who joins himself to a religious society does so presumably because of benefits which are expected to accrue. The group relationship possesses value to him. In the case of the early Christians the value is readily evident,[2] as it is today in the less sophisticated religious groups, in the supernaturalistic world-view which obtained. Such matters as eternal bliss, eternal punishment, salvation, communion with the deity, the transformation from the "old" to the "new" status, and other concepts of a like nature were values whose reality not only was unquestioned but was vividly pictured in specific imagery.

This being true, it follows that the maintenance of the group relation was also important. To put it otherwise, the loss of relationship, of identity with the group, was serious. To be sure, joining the early Christian group appears to have entailed the severance of relation with such other religious groups as the adherent had formerly belonged to, but this itself implies an evaluation; it was in such case judged that the relation to the Christian group

[1] Cf. Coe, *The Psychology of Religion* (Chicago, 1916), pp. 126–32.

[2] Case, *The Social Origins of Christianity* (Chicago, 1924).

was of such superior worth that the change of affiliation was warranted. As has been urged, the issue of persecution was a conflict of loyalties between a grouping approved by the state and, on the other hand, groups which, though they were in the minority, nevertheless possessed sufficient sustaining power that adherence to them was thought to be warranted in the face of disapproval, punishment, or even death.

Obviously, the projection of such an idea witnesses to the influence of the Christian groups upon their adherents. Large numbers of persons were convinced of the worth of belonging to Christian churches. They submitted to the authority of officials, who from an early date insisted upon the maintenance of regularity in church rites and the effectiveness of church discipline. They gradually developed customs peculiarly their own, so that their religious societies presently possessed individuality and distinction from other more or less similar groups. Their customs grew into norms and ultimately into rules. Sanctions were given as literature grew up and attained the status of canonicity. Nothing is clearer than the attempt on the part of the Christian public to come to terms with the Empire, and their insistence, in their literature of defense, of the propriety of their undisturbed existence. Success in extending their number implies success in imposing their patterns, and, of course, the adoption by adherents of Christian standards and manners.

The basis of the control of their adherents by Christian groups in situations of persecution did not essentially differ from the basis of their control in other relationships. The most important factor in determining the basis of control was the expansion of the Christian movement into the Western world. This marked the abandonment of the possibility that Christianity might ever be an oriental religion, and meant, instead, that its membership would be made up of those subjects of the Roman Empire among whom many syncretistic religions had been brought into prominence. The ultimate meaning of this factor is that the control of Christian adherents was upon that basis which obtained in the psychology of the Graeco-Roman public during the Hellenistic period.

The religious societies of the Western world have always been noted for their success in controlling the individual by means of the group. Such a method has obtained because of the prevalent basis in the individualism which has been characteristic of Western society in certain periods. One such epoch was that which was brought into being by the events centering around the achievements of Alexander.[1] The period of Hellenism was a time when, the previously existing city-states and nations having fallen, there emerged the recognition of the ultimate value of the person as such. This was the natural, the inevitable, result of the obliteration of previously existing city and national barriers. The

[1] Case, *The Evolution of Early Christianity* (Chicago, 1914), pp. 48–77.

fall of the city-state and the wiping-out of the national lines effectually removed the basis for aught
but the rarely attempted Stoic ideal of world-
citizenship or the generally prevalent individualism.

The individualism which was so characteristic a
feature of the Hellenistic period was, of course,
simply the opposite of the previously existing national or civic groupings. It does not imply the denial of the validity of social influence or control. It
merely marks the necessity, in the face of the general breakdown of the social organizations which
had been familiar, of reorganization, of reintegra-
tion into such social groupings as became possible
in the new world.

Hellenistic individualism may readily be seen in
the religious quest which was satisfied by the Hellenistic religious cults. National cults no longer
guaranteed "salvation," the present and future welfare for which need was so poignantly felt. One born
in Egypt and sold as a slave to Ephesus could no
longer depend upon the gods of his native land to
protect him; apart from home and kindred, he had
to be assured of religious satisfactions, of protection
and welfare, of "salvation" of himself as a person.
The Syrian resident in Alexandria must completely
reorganize his religious conceptions. The local gods
had proved to be unequal to the task of maintaining the old world-order, and a new world demanded
new religious conceptions.

The response to this need came in the many Hel-

lenistic religions of redemption.[1] If the person was
thrown back upon the consciousness of his need as
such, the redemption cults assured him of his salvation as such. He was assured that he was saved,
without reference to his race, his nation, his city.
It was not because he was an Athenian, or what not,
that he was saved, but because Isis or Cybele or
Jesus had redeemed him. The ultimate unit of value
in the characteristic Hellenism of the Graeco-Roman period was the person himself, or, as he is usually called, the individual.

It was as Wendland says:

Individualism is just as characteristic of the Hellenistic
age as is cosmopolitanism. The latter does not exclude the
former; it is rather the most suitable soil for the growth of it.
The barriers that so far state, society, and religion have set
for the individual have loosened and fallen. The individual
acquires liberty to live for himself. . . . . It is a time of liber-
ated individuality, the time in which the consequences of an
individualistic current beginning with sophism are nurtured.
This new frame of mind, the firm belief in the right and the
meaning of personality, dominates Hellenistic philosophy.
In the philosophies of this age practical-ethical matters pre-
dominate, and ethics is individual.[2]

It was therefore but natural for the emerging
Christian groups, as they made progress in their
expansion throughout the Western world, to find
themselves in adaptation of such a current social

[1] Case, *ibid.*, pp. 284–330.

[2] Wendland, *Die Hellenistisch-römische Kultur in Ihren Beziehungen zu
Judentum und Christentum* (Tübingen, 1907), pp. 19 f.

attitude. It is because the new movement, like other Hellenistic redemption cults, responded to the current social attitude that it became characteristically a non-nationalistic, non-racial movement. It was an entirely natural corollary that as the Christian groups found it necessary to organize their techniques of control they developed the methods by which the groups controlled the individuals who formed the groups.

The control of the individual by the group to which he belonged was in stark contrast to the techniques by which the nationalistic basis of the earlier oriental religions had been preserved. To be sure, Judaism is the sole important exception to the otherwise complete breakdown of the racial-national religions in the Hellenistic age. With this important exception the plan of Alexander succeeded to an astonishing degree, although its details were perforce carried out by succeeding generations. The implications of the process for religion were great indeed, as the rapid transformation of the Graeco-Roman world shows. Christianity was but a part of the total movement which was the inevitable result of the new social trends which came into being in the Hellenistic age.

The utilization of this characteristic social attitude by Christian societies is most effectively seen as it is contrasted with the methods of control in non-individualistic groups. The experiences of Judaism in persecution may be studied quite usefully. The persecutions suffered by Judiasm did not essentially differ from those of the Christians. But the basis of control, and consequently the techniques and methods, were altogether different in the two cases. The Christian groups controlled their adherents by appealing to the single person, while Jewish social groups emphasized the necessity of maintaining the integrity of the racial-national unit, and never utilized any of the implications of the social attitude of individualism.

The difference of basis, with consequent difference in techniques and methods of control, may readily be observed in examples of persecution in the history of Judaism which are reflected in the several specimens of literature which the persecutions brought into existence. The revolution which followed the attempt of Antiochus IV to force the Hellenization of his subjects, the conflicts between Sadducees and Pharisees during the period immediately preceding the Roman occupation of Palestine, the cases of warfare during the Roman period, and the many occasions of the persecution of Jews by Christians have all produced Jewish martyrs of no less fortitude than was exhibited by Christian saints.

It is easy to see the reflex of these experiences in the literature:

How many persecutions have been decreed against Israel, but they have given their lives for the Sanctification of the Name.[1]

Why goest thou forth to be killed by the sword? Because I

[1] Midrash Tillim on Psalm 18:7.

circumcised my son. Why goest thou forth to be burned? Because I read the Torah. Why goest thou forth to be crucified? Because I ate unleavened bread.[1]

If you are asked to give your life for the Sanctification of the Name, say, "I am ready to give it, only may I be beheaded at once, and not be tortured as in the days of persecution."[2]

What did they do in the generation of the persecution? They took iron balls and made them white hot and put them under their armpits, and took away their lives from them, and they brought sharp reeds and put them under their nails, and so they died for the Sanctification of the Name.[3]

But Palestinian Judaism, as a racial-national religion, when faced with the task of controlling its adherents, followed methods which differed from those utilized by Christian leaders, the difference being caused by the totally different basis upon which control was projected. The Christians maintained the integrity of their groups by directing control to the individual, while Judaism consistently effected control by appealing to the group as such. It was the unit to which control was directed that differed.

The reason, of course, was that Judaism possessed a racial-national basis, as Christianity did not. The Jews were a people, as the Christians were not.[4] Indeed, it may be affirmed that the maintenance of Jewish nationalism, without the political or military machinery of state, is one of the most remark-

[1] Sotah 31a.

[2] Pesikta C:x:87a.   [3] Midrash Tillim on Psalm 16:3.

[4] Bigelmair, *Die Beteiligung der Christen am öffentlichen Leben in vorconstantinischer Zeit* (München, 1902), p. 26.

able achievements in the entire range of social control. At all events, Judaism by means of its particular methods of control has preserved its integrity, even in the face of persecution which exceeded in severity and continuity the anti-Christian activities of the Roman state.

As has been noted, Judaism was the sole exception of importance to the otherwise complete breakdown of nationalism which occurred as the conquests of Alexander brought Hellenism into being. Unlike other religious groups, it depended primarily upon a racial relationship. It consistently demanded of one of another race or religious fellowship who desired to join Judaism that he join the Jewish race. This, of course, is the significance of the circumcision of proselytes. It does not appear that additions to Judaism by proselyting were very numerous. On the other hand, the leavening effect of Jewish life was always of great effect. What is essential in understanding this important difference between Judaism and the Hellenistic religions, of which Christianity was one, is that Judaism never went far in adapting itself to the social attitude of individualism which was so characteristic of the Hellenistic world. Palestinian Judaism, indeed, forms almost no exception to this statement. It was only in certain particulars that Hellenistic Judaism exhibits modification in this direction; and in the ultimate point, that of the maintenance of racial-national integrity, it, no more than Palestinian Judaism, was unwavering.

Judaism thus offers an instructive contrast to Christianity in the matter of the technique of control in persecution. The two points of view may readily be seen in the literatures of persecution which were produced by the respective movements. As has been pointed out, the characteristic type of Christian writing in persecution was the martyrology. In Judaism, on the other hand, it was the apocalypse which presently functioned to meet the situations of persecution. Examples are numerous.[1] From the persecution of Antiochus IV came the canonical apocalypse of Daniel, and, it appears, part of the composite work known as I Enoch. From the civil conflicts of Jewish groups came other sections of I Enoch. From the earlier Roman period may be mentioned the Assumption of Moses. As the zealot propaganda arose and the first Roman assault upon Jerusalem occurred, there were written the parts of the composite work which is called by the name of Baruch. The troubled time of Domitian apparently left its impress upon Jewish writing as it did upon Christian, since with the New Testament apocalypse may be compared that perfect example of the type, IV Ezra.

The apocalypse, like the martyrology, had for its purpose the maintenance of the integrity of the religious group from whose point of view it was written. It, also like the martyrology, utilized sanctions of reward and punishment to secure its end.

[1] In the matter of dating and analysis of the apocalypses, Charles, *Apocrypha and Pseudepigrapha*, is followed.

But in method of control comparison is replaced by contrast. The most telling difference occurs in the imagery of reward. As has been shown, the martyrology pictured the successful hero as immediately enjoying heavenly bliss. He is now reigning with Christ, and shall reign for ever and ever. This value is urged in the terms, familiar in Greek thought, of personal immortality. But the apocalypse couches its imagery of heavenly bliss only in terms of the Jewish resurrection faith: he who becomes a martyr rather than forego his faith survives the judgment, and in the great resurrection he becomes one of the glorious company of the apocalyptic kingdom of God. This, of course, is a social concept. It was never urged that the martyr might be blessed apart from his fellows. It was assumed that his blessedness would be realized only in the common life. The apocalypse functioned to maintain the identity of the individual with his group, and it did so by reiterating that only apostasy might cause the loss of status, that even though death might intervene the social values of the religious group would be preserved in the kingdom of God.

The apocalypse as a literary type had its psychology,[1] as did the martyrology. Coming as it did from situations of persecution, it is not remarkable that the basic element in the apocalypse is the reflection of emotional seizures. In it the writer is pictured as having, through the gift of prophecy, fore-

[1] Riddle, "The Physical Basis of Apocalypticism," *Journal of Religion*, IV (1924), 174–91.

seen dreadful experiences. The visions through which these were foreseen are told for prophylactic effect; opportunity is thus given for conveying the message of the work. Always they are expressed with every gradation of fear, horror, and dread, but always with the unpleasant experiences balanced by visions in which future blessedness is assured with promises of joy, peace, and contentment.

But even in the frankest exhibition of emotion another contrast with the martyrology is apparent. As was noted, the masochistic impulse which was present in the martyrologist led him to picture the torture of the martyrs with considerable morbid pleasure. But there is no such abnormal satisfaction in suffering reflected in the apocalypses. There is no concealing the dread of the pain. It may fairly be generalized that the apocalypse reveals a more healthy mind than does the martyrology.

The apocalypse in Judaism was utilized by a particular group, and its production was confined to Palestinian situations. Dispersion Judaism, as it suffered from persecution, exhibits a certain adaptation toward the social attitudes which were characteristic of the Hellenistic world. This may be seen in the fact that the type of persecution literature produced in Hellenistic Judaism correlates with the martyrologies rather than with the apocalypses. The persecution literature of Hellenistic Judaism exhibits the effect of environmental influences. Again, the fact may be readily observed in examples. The Maccabean books immediately occur to mind. First Maccabees is not significant in the present connection, since it was of the Palestinian milieu and was written from a group standpoint which gives it character irrelevant to the subject of investigation. Second, Third, and Fourth Maccabees, however, are highly instructive. It requires but cursory survey to detect that these are not apocalypses, but, on the other hand, that they conform to the martyrological type. In them the interest is highly individualistic, and the effort is made to picture heroic acts in all their harrowing details. In other words, they are practically martyrologies. What is important for the present study is that their psychological and literary relationships are with Greek literature. Even though their authors were Jewish by race, the works show unquestionably that in this matter Hellenistic Judaism, in clear distinction from Palestinian, was strongly affected by the Hellenistic social attitudes which so powerfully influenced Christianity.

In the same direction the traces of persecution in the rabbinical literature may be cited. They, too, support the generalization which is taking shape. This literature is not apocalyptic. It is interesting to note that in it the traces of data on persecution are of the individualistic, rather than of the social, correlation. Schürer[1] has pointed out that, while in the older parts of this literature, occasional reference is made to the martyr death of a rabbi, it is only in the midrashim of the post-Talmudic period

[1] Schürer, *A History of the Jewish People* (Leipzig, 1901), I, ii, 313.

that such stories are gathered together, i.e., after Judaism had become chiefly an extra-Palestinian movement, with utter loss of national existence. Another matter of curious import is that, as Juster[1] has pointed out, the destruction of Judaism, which figured so importantly in the apocalypses, would be unknown in detail from the rabbinical sources, while hardly more is to be learned from them of the war of Hadrian.

Perhaps the most telling illustration of the tendency which so clearly emphasizes the difference between the apocalyptic and the non-apocalyptic attitudes toward martyrdom is the story of the death of Akiba, which is told with graphic detail in the Jerusalem Talmud.[2] It is well worth repeating: R. Akiba was at the point of death under torture by Turnus Rufus when the moment of repeating the Shema arrived. He began its repetition with a smile. The torturer asked if he was a sorcerer, to be able to smile at such a moment. The faithful rabbi replied, "All my life I have recited this verse, and it has always caused me chagrin. . . . . I have proved that I love God with all my heart and with all my strength, but not until now have I proved that I love him with all my life"; and while saying this he died. This story might fittingly have stood in any martyrology.

Similar, and almost equally effective for the purpose of control, are the stories told in the Macca-

[1] Juster, *Les juifs dans l'empire romain* (Paris, 1913), I, 22.

[2] TJ Berakhoth 97.

bean books of the death of Eleazar. As first told in
II Maccabees, the tale exhibits a notable adaptation to Hellenistic influences. But as retold in the
highly literary and rhetorical account of IV Maccabees, the advance in the development of martyrological purpose is striking (II Macc. 6:18–31; IV
Macc. 5:16 ff.). The same is to be said about the
double accounts of the torture of the mother and
her seven sons (II Macc. 7:1–42; IV Macc. 8:1 ff.).

It is a significant illustration of the basis of control that, although the social basis of the apocalypse
marks its literary type as distinctive, the martyrological interest in the literature of Hellenistic
Judaism conforms to the psychological and literary
canons of its environment. The distinctive feature
of the apocalypses, their social basis, differs in kind
from the individualistic basis of control which is apparent in the martyr stories of Hellenistic Judaism,
which so perfectly correlate with the Christian
types. Even Schlatter, who attempts to demonstrate that the Christian literature of persecution
depends upon Jewish sources, admits this, stating
that II Maccabees and the history of Jason of
Cyrene which it epitomizes belong to Greek literature and are influenced by Greek motives.[1] He also
refers to the fact that the preservation of II and IV
Maccabees was due to the synagogues of the Greek
world.[2] This marks a clean-cut distinction, for the

[1] Schlatter, *Die Märtyrer in den Anfängen der Kirche* (Gütersloh, 1915),
p. 13.
[2] *Ibid.*, p. 51.

apocalypses were not preserved by the Greek synagogues.[1] Josephus, too, conforms to the fundamental differentia;[2] in the Greek manner and for a
Graeco-Roman public he celebrates the occasions in
which the prizes of martyrdom were won by certain
of his compatriots. Significantly, Josephus is not an
apocalyptist.

The distinction in social attitudes is thus apparent in its fully worked-out extremes; what is even
more instructive is to observe the steps in the process of differentiation. As is well known, there was a
period in the emergence of Christianity when its
public was Jewish and when a number of its churches
were situated in Palestine. As might be expected
from the fact of this relationship, the earlier Christian literature is considerably impregnated with
apocalypticism. Not only Paul as one of the earlier
leaders was an apocalyptist, but the Synoptic Gospels in varying degree contain apocalyptic materials. The Revelation of John as a complete book of
the New Testament is apocalyptic in character.
Obviously, in its early stage the emerging movement shared the social point of view of Judaism.

But equally clearly, as Christianity became at
home in the Western world it underwent a transi-
tion in which, as it became a non-nationalistic redemption cult, offering salvation to the individual,
it adopted the current Hellenistic attitude of individualism. In the process the adaptation to Hel-

---

[1] Burkitt, *Jewish and Christian Apocalypses* (London, 1914), pp. 15 f.

[2] Schlatter, *op. cit.*, p. 15.

lenistic thought-processes gradually caused the abandonment of those relations with Judaism which formerly had influenced the movement. It is thus that the disuse of apocalyptic in Christianity, and the substitution for it of a different type of control literature, is to be understood.[1]

To be sure, this process was not sudden, nor was it altogether without exception. Certain of the Christian leaders who wrote on persecution used apocalyptic conceptions. Tertullian combined strong apocalyptic tendencies with an ardent attitude toward martyrdom. Cyprian used apocalyptic terms. One of the apocalyptic ideas, that a catastrophic end of the age would occur after a thousand years, was maintained until a relatively late date. However, apocalyptic, or more properly chiliastic, thinking soon exhibited modifications as the church became integrated into society;[2] the church presently took the place of the kingdom of God imagery, until it was commonly thought that it was a permanently established organism. The social unit became the church rather than the catastrophically instituted kingdom of God. In this process apocalypticism was abandoned.

At the time that the martyrologies flourished, the process was at its mid-point. At the same time that certain leaders used apocalyptic imagery, the indi-

---

[1] Riddle, "From Apocalypse to Martyrology," *Anglican Theological Review*, IX (1927), 260–80.

[2] Edwards, *The Transformation of Early Christianity from an Eschatological to a Social Movement* (Menasha, Wisconsin, 1919).

vidualistic attitude toward martyrdom was becoming current. Thus, as might be expected, the later apocalypses produced by Christians became tinctured by the Hellenistic influences.[1] As, presently, they exhibit the influence of the attitude of individualism, the volume of martyrologies greatly exceeds the production of apocalypses, and the transformation from apocalypse to martyrology is well under way. Commentaries upon previously existing apocalypses were written rather than additional revelations.[2] The full fruit of the tendency may be seen in such a writer as Origen, who had an abundance of materials from which apocalypses might have been written, but who, thoroughly integrated into the thought-patterns of his place and time, wrote instead one of the most fervid of the exhortations to martyrdom. The matter is well put by Bigelmair: "Rigorism in the tendency of the time fell back upon itself. Apocalyptic ideas declined."[3]

The effect of the process upon the Christian apocalypses is interesting. Subsequent to the composition of those apocalyptic materials which found their way into the New Testament two others which did not enjoy that fate were produced. These exhibit plainly the effects of the transformation. Both of these, the *Shepherd* of Hermas and the

---

[1] See below, pp. 169 f.

[2] Eusebius *Church History* vi. 7; cf. Bonwetsch, *Studien zu den Kommentaren Hippolyts zum buche Daniel und Hohenliede;* Gebhardt, Harnack, and Zahn, *Texte und Untersuchungen*, I, ii, 1–86.

[3] Bigelmair, *op. cit.*, pp. 14 f.

Apocalypse of Peter, were used by the writers of martyrologies, doubtless because, unlike the true apocalypses, they are more Hellenistic than Jewish.

This may be seen, for example, in their imagery of heaven and hell. Geffcken calls attention to the relation of these concepts to the Orphic-Pythagorean influences;[1] and Dieterich, with special reference to the so-called Apocalypse of Peter, goes so far as to say that the characteristics properly belonging to the Jewish apocalypses are absent without a trace.[2]

It would require but the merest glance at the *Shepherd* of Hermas to see in it the typical Western attitude toward suffering in persecution. Since the work is not well known, it may not be amiss to illustrate the point by a citation:

What, said I, did they bear? . . . . Stripes, imprisonments, great afflictions, crucifixions, wild beasts, for the sake of the Name. Therefore it is given to them to be on the right hand of holiness, and to everyone who shall suffer for the Name. . . . . As many as ever suffered for the Name are glorious before God, and the sins of all these have been taken away because they suffered for the Name of the son of God. . . . . As many as were brought under authority and were questioned and did not deny, but suffered readily, these are especially glorious before the Lord . . . . [*ibid. Vision* 3:1:9—3:2:1].

It may indeed be said that the *Shepherd* has proceeded far enough in the transformation that it is

---

[1] Geffcken, *Aus den Werdezeit des Christentums* (Leipzig, 1909), p. 56.

[2] Dieterich, *Nekyia: Beiträge zur Erklärung der Neuentdekten Petrus-apokalypse* (Leipzig, 1893), p. 222.

hardly an apocalypse at all. It uses the mode of revelation as the vehicle by which its messages are expressed, but it is an apocalypse strictly speaking only in so far as it uses revelation as epistemological method.[1]

Other steps in the transformation include the working-over by Christians of typical Jewish apocalypses, modifying them in the directions by which they might be made useful for Christian methods of control. Perhaps the most obvious example is the Christian form of the Ascension of Isaiah, with its strong reflection of the untoward events of Nero's reign and its almost explicit reference to the martyrdom of Peter (Asc. Isa. 4:1 ff.). Another less familiar work is the Jewish Sibyl, which in its worked-over form pictures the destruction of the Temple, the suppression of Christians by Nero, and the Nero-*redivivus* myth (Sib. Or. 3:63–75; 4:15–27; 4:130; 5:30, 42, 63 ff.). Similarly, but with hardly the same interests, the Enoch and Baruch apocalypses were interpolated. Greek influences in the description of heaven and hell are apparent in the later apocalypse of Enoch, known as II Enoch.

There is thus no mistaking the modifications of the types of literature used for the purpose of control in persecution. Nor may one fail to see that these modifications were due to the different environmental influences of Hellenistic and Palestinian patterns of thought and expression, resting ul-

[1] Riddle, "The Messages of the Shepherd of Hermas, A Study in Social Control," *Journal of Religion*, VII (1927), 561–77.

timately upon differing social attitudes. The martyrologies to a certain extent used the apocalyptic concepts as inherited dogma, and certain vestigial features of the apocalyptic elements remained for a time in use among Christians; but the transference from the social basis to the individualistic, from the idea of the ultimate value of the group to the idea of the superior value of the individual, entailed a corollary. The two literatures show that Palestinian Judaism in control in persecution appealed to the group, while the Christians for the same purpose directed their appeal to a different basis, namely, to the individual.

Criteria indicating the change are readily observable: the thought of personal immortality rather than the idea of the resurrection of the individual with his group, the morbid desire for suffering as distinct from the normal attitude reflected in the apocalypse, the picture in the martyrologies of a hero of the present age as against the convention in apocalyptic writing of putting the messages of the writer as though they were the revelations of a notable person of the glorious past. These and like elements are features of two worlds and of two literatures. To be sure, the aim of both types was control in persecution, but their conception of task significantly differed as each projected its technique upon a differing basis of control.

The basis upon which Christian leaders developed their techniques and methods of control was thus the same social attitude of individualism which characterized Christianity in other respects. It was this which crystallized and answered the issue as some early leaders demanded that new adherents to the churches must be circumcised. It was because the new movement developed as a non-national, a non-racial cult that its policy was inevitable. The answer which was made carried with it the far-reaching consequence that Christianity was to become a cult of the redemption of the individual, as other Hellenistic cults were non-nationalistic and non-racial. Judaism remained the sole exception of importance to the otherwise general breakdown of nationalism in the religions of the Hellenistic world. Thus seen, the difference in the basis to which control in persecution was applied is perfectly logical.

It appears, moreover, that in its adoption of the characteristics of the Hellenistic cults Christianity went much farther than the mere adoption of an individualistic conception of redemption. Without doubt its adoption of this current concept had much to do with its well-nigh complete absorption into itself of practically all the religious interests of the Graeco-Roman world.

It is in point again to refer to the Christian attitude toward martyrdom and the current attitude as reflected in the familiar hero cult. As has been urged above, it was by no accident that the cult of the martyr developed upon the soil which had been prepared by the earlier and contemporary Greek cults of hero gods, of gods who became divine after having as men attained unusual status by reason of their heroic deeds. The ease with which heroic behavior in suffering martyrdom became rewarded with veneration in the martyr cult is thus explicable.

Again, the assimilation by Christians of many of the local divinities from the religions of their contemporaries is a factor closely connected with the cult of the martyr. The obvious example, of course, is the survival as saints of the Christian calendar many of the healing divinities of such localities as southern Italy and Spain. The operation of the process suggests the ease with which the martyr cult developed in surroundings where the hero stood out as a notable individual.

It must therefore be concluded that the current attitude of individualism was the effective cause in Christianity's directing its control to the individual as the basis. It could not have been otherwise, the social attitudes being as they were. It was upon this basis that techniques and methods were developed. Perhaps the practical application was with more or less *naïveté*, but it was not less effective for that reason. The process was one which is immensely instructive as it is seen in its perspective and in contrast with other observable developments.

VII

SOME EARLIER SITUATIONS

It is tolerably clear that the early Christians met situations of persecution by developing methods of social control. It has been shown that the survival of the Christian movement was due to its successful resistance of the state and to its persistent refusal to conform to approved religious patterns. However, the conspicuous success of Christianity in social control occurred as the issue of persecution was perfectly clear, so that techniques were developed to meet it. But such was the case only when persecution was clearly understood by the Christian leaders, who were thus able to meet it by calculated procedure.

As has been pointed out, the first of the persecutions which may properly be called such was that of Decius. It is surprising that the first came so late. To be sure, it was fortunate for the Christians that it was thus late, for the progress of the rising movement was such that in the somewhat over two centuries preceding, the competition of Christian groups with the religious parties represented in state opposition was not too unequal to be without hope of success.

There were, of course, earlier situations which in tradition have been regarded and denominated as persecutions. Strict accuracy demands that they be more correctly defined. They were either of such local limitation or of such brief duration that suppression or coercion are better terms. Some, indeed, may be regarded as no more than mob actions. Clearly it is not in keeping with strict accuracy to dignify them by placing them in the category of persecution. Not that accuracy in terminology is of ultimate importance. What is important is that these earlier situations, brief in duration, limited in application to particular localities, or lacking in premeditated purpose or method, did not present the Christians or groups of Christians concerned with an issue which was sufficiently familiar to be met with concerted effort, which was planned on the basis of known experience.

Such was the case, for example, in that rapid and savage attack upon the Christians of Lyons and Vienne. In that horrid situation martyrs were made, but so obviously was the event the fortuitous or adventitious expression of mob passion that calculated opposition was not to be thought of. The confessors were making history, not profiting by it. The martyrs became heroes, but they themselves were unaware of the significance of their behavior.

Or, again, much the same must be said of the actions which caused the death of those several in Smyrna of whom Polycarp is the most famous martyr. These events, particularly those concerning Polycarp himself, were indeed coolly ordered by the officials, and some regard was had for legal procedure; but even so, it is apparent that Polycarp was, in comparison with many subsequent martyrs, without the benefit of known examples of behavior under such circumstances. His heroic behavior became ideal and in Christian desire typical, but it was not typical at the time for the simple reason that there was no type.

Justin and his associates, or the group of Scillitan martyrs, were also unfortunate victims of situations not yet general enough to be regarded as familiar. These persons, famed by their followers, were in doubtful status. The alternative which they faced was genuine, for, with much less of known values to control them, they might certainly have denied. That they rather confessed is to their credit, of course, and doubly so in view of the inability of the groups to which they belonged to furnish backing in their moment of need.

How early may the development of technique be observed? The question assumes the greater importance when it is recognized that some of the earlier situations antedate the composition of certain of the New Testament sources. To what extent does the New Testament, the earliest literature of Christianity, reflect attitudes toward "persecution"? What does it offer with reference to the development of methods for meeting such situations?

Students of the New Testament are accustomed to the association of the Book of Revelation with the so-called "persecution" of Domitian. There is an increasing consensus that its message is understood only as the book is read in the light of that background. But it is not to be supposed that this is the sole example of the influence of coercive activity upon the New Testament. The so-called First Epistle of Peter is quite commonly found to have its message shaped by such influence. It is questionable only whether the particular "persecution" involved is that of Domitian or of Trajan. With the alleged persecution of Domitian is also related the Epistle to the Hebrews. Further, it is a matter likely to be important that the Gospel according to Mark was written not far from the time when certain Christians were said to have suffered during Nero's reign. Nero's fell influence is also to be found in the Book of Revelation.

It is an interesting fact that, while the New Testament was being written, at least two situations of suppression occurred which are reflected in specimens of Christian writing which, although they antedate some of the books of the New Testament, were not included in its collection. There are several letters written by Ignatius, bishop of Antioch in Syria, who was martyred in Rome sometime during the reign of Trajan (A.D. 98–117), perhaps in 108. These letters are highly instructive, exhibiting exactly that ardent desire for martyrdom which has been noted as characteristic of some of the more nearly abnormal cases. While Ignatius was not under the jurisdiction of Pliny, whose letters to the Emperor at about the same time are so important, his references to his experience valuably supplement not only Pliny's information but the data of the New Testament as well.

A second example is furnished by the letter of the Roman church to the Corinthians, generally known as First Clement. This source, which by many is regarded as having been written at the time of Domitian's suppression, refers explicitly to the untoward events through which the group had passed, and celebrates as already recognized models the martyrs Peter and Paul. In the case of I Clement relation with the New Testament is particularly close. Not only does the work come from the time of the suppression of Domitian, but it has been regarded as likely that it actually called forth the writing of the Epistle to the Hebrews.[1]

It is apparent, then, that the development of typical attitudes toward martyrdom was a process which may be traced to times as early as the production of the New Testament. It is necessary, indeed, in studying the phenomena of control in persecution to canvass the reflections of these earlier situations in order to determine their contribution to the methods which enabled the Christian groups to win in their apparently unequal contest with the state, and to learn, if possible, how control was effected before the well-known methods were fully developed.

There is reflected in the New Testament a situa-

---

[1] Goodspeed, *New Solutions of New Testament Problems* (Chicago, 1927), pp. 110–15; Riddle, "Hebrews, First Clement, and the Persecution of Domitian," *Journal of Biblical Literature*, XLIII (1924), 329–48.

tion of persecution which is of uncertain date. The
so-called Pastoral Epistles clearly exhibit the presence of a consciousness of the value of martyrdom.
These letters, bearing the name of Paul, are now
widely recognized as pseudonymous. However this
may be, it is not basically relevant for the present
study, but it is essential that the letters be observed
as reflecting the typical attitude toward martyrdom. The reader is exhorted to "fight the good fight
of faith" since he had already "confessed the good
confession in the sight of many martyrs" (I Tim.
6:12). Jesus is already the great example, "who before Pontius Pilate witnessed the good confession"
(*ibid.* 6:13).

Clearly in the later literature on martyrdom the
terms "confess" and "martyr" (or "witness") possessed technical meaning. When did they attain it?
Now, if modern scholarship is correct in its judgment that the Pastoral Epistles use Paul's name
pseudonymously, and in its dating of them near the
middle of the second century, they are not far from
the time when typical martyrologies were being
written. In view of this it is striking that there is
an almost exact parallel to the terminology of
I Timothy in an early martyrology. In the Acts of
Justin one Paeon says: "I received this good confession from my parents" (*ibid.* 4:6). The work
closes with the statement that "the holy martyrs
.... fulfilled their testimony [μαρτυρίαν] by the
confession [ὁμολογία] of the Savior" (6:1). It is in
related meaning that the story of Polycarp tells of

the thrice heralded announcement: "Polycarp has confessed himself to be a Christian." First Timothy's language uses the figure of fighting; in like manner the story of the Scillitan martyrs, not far distant in date, associates confession with fighting (*Acts of the Scillitan Martyrs* 17). The somewhat later source which tells of the martyrs of Lyons and Vienne abounds with usage of the terms "confess," "confession," and "struggle" (Eusebius *Church History* v. 1, *passim*). It is quite fair to say that by the time of I Timothy's writing the terminology of control in persecution had become technical.

In the same source the citation of Jesus as a martyr who had confessed before Pilate shows also that the use of the passion story as authoritative, to induce the desired attitude toward martyrdom, which was so effective later, was already normative. The story of Polycarp's death refers to this martyrdom as one "according to the Gospel" (*Martyrdom of Polycarp* i. 1). To illustrate the claim many parallels to the passion of Jesus are consciously cited.[1] True, in I Timothy the item is not highly developed, but there is no question that its use of Jesus as a model marks a stage in the process of developing technique in control in persecution.

Possibly the careful identification of Jesus as "the blessed and only Sovereign, King of kings and Lord of lords" (I Tim. 6:15) is made with conscious reference to the cult of the emperor, which was fre-

---

[1] Riddle, "A Literary Allusion in the Martyrdom of Polycarp," *Anglican Theological Review*, VIII (1925), 136–42.

quently the cause of Christian martyrdoms. Such seems to have been true in the situation basic to the New Testament Apocalypse, and was clearly true in the action referred to in Pliny's letter to Trajan. Discrimination between Jesus as Lord and the lord of the Empire figures in the early martyrologies. Polycarp, when asked what harm there is in saying "Caesar is Lord," replies, "How can I blaspheme my King who saved me?" (*Martyrdom of Polycarp* ix. 3). The Scillitan martyrs, when required to swear by the emperor's genius, severally reply that they "do not recognize the empire of this age" but the "Lord, the King of kings and Emperor of all peoples." They "honor Caesar as Caesar, but fear God" (*Acts of the Scillitan Martyrs* 2, 3, 6, 9). It is likely that I Timothy reflects a stage of development in which the cult of the emperor appears in relation to the growing methods of control.

Second Timothy, also, reflects a situation which was instructive in times of persecution. In it, for example, Paul is made to refer to his own suffering as exemplary, and from them to conclude that "all who would live godly in Christ Jesus shall suffer persecution (II Tim. 3:10–12). The reader is exhorted to "endure hardship as a good soldier of Christ Jesus" (2:3), and the exhortation carries figures which were avidly used by the later literature on martyrdom: the sufferer is an athlete who is crowned. Polycarp was said to have been "crowned with the crown of immortality" and to have "won a prize beyond gainsaying" (*Martyrdom of Polycarp* xvii. 1); and not only all the Lyons and Vienne martyrs were called athletes (Eusebius *Church History* v. 1. 36), but individuals severally are celebrated as such, even the woman, Blandina (*ibid.* v. 1. 19).

One of the most striking features of II Timothy is the use made of song in inducing the attitude of willingness to undergo martyrdom. The famous example is 2:11–13:

> If we have died with him, we shall live with him,
> If we endure, we shall also reign with him,
> If we deny, he also shall deny us,
> If we are unfaithful, that one shall remain faithful,
> For he cannot deny himself!

It has been noted that song became one of the elements of church discipline by which indoctrination was effected and emotional appeal engendered. How interesting that so early an example is available! All this terminology became technical in the martyrologies.

But the most important element of the so-called Pastoral Epistles in the light of martyrological data is their claim to function as letters of Paul and their supply of autobiographical details of the same hero. Thus, the letters do not merely exhort that one fight the good fight of faith, but furnish a telling example: "I have fought the good fight, I have finished the course, I have kept the faith." Consequently there is implicit trust in the reward: "Henceforth there is laid up for me the crown of righteousness, which the Lord, the righteous judge, shall give to me in that day, and not to me only, but also to them that have loved his appearing" (II Tim. 4:7–8). The function of such matter as this is best seen in the light of the literature of martyrdom, in which the similar purpose leads to the citation of apostolic or other heroic examples. Paul seems, in spite of the early tradition of his martyrdom, to have suffered an eclipse during the second century. The Pastorals apparently are designed to assist in his rehabilitation. It is an interesting fact that the purpose of control in a situation of something like persecution was the effective motive of their celebration of his heroism.

The second of the earlier situations of suppression which are reflected in early Christian literature may, it is thought, be dated. It stands next in the series. Taking the Pastoral Epistles, though they may not be definitely dated, as not far in time from those untoward actions which occurred during the periods of Marcus Aurelius and Antonius Pius (reflected in the letter of the Christians of Lyons and Vienne, the Martyrdom of Polycarp, the Acts of the Scillitan Martyrs, and the Acts of Justin), the next such action of which there is information is that which occurred under Trajan's administration and is so well reflected in the letter of Pliny. The proposition has been capably stated, and given exposition, that the New Testament document known as the First Epistle of Peter comes from the so-called "persecution" of Trajan.[1]

[1] Case, "Peter, Epistles of," in Hastings' *Dictionary of the Apostolic Church*, II, 201–9.

To be sure, a larger group of scholars hold that I Peter came from the period of Domitian.[1] But there is a datum in the letter and in the two situations, which, it appears, is decisive. This is the legal basis for the actions in which Christians were involved. Clearly, it was not until Pliny's letter and Trajan's reply that anyone was liable to suffer simply because he was a Christian. As shall be shown, that which involved Christians into trouble during Domitian's time was their repudiation of the cult of the emperor; one suffered then because he refused to acknowledge Domitian to be Lord, not necessarily because he was a Christian. Presumably his being a Christian was not notable until he refused to comply with the manners of the imperial cult. It was first during the reign of Trajan that being a Christian was decreed to be a crime as such. Previously the crime of being a member of an illegal religious group had to be made overt by such a clash of cult observance as was exemplified by the troubles in Asia which precipitated the Book of Revelation.

But I Peter shows that the mere name of Christian might bring one to court. The public of this letter had been "for a little while . . . . put to grief in manifold trials" (I Pet. 4:14). It is plainly stated that they are likely to be "reproached for the name of Christ" (4:16). One might indeed "suffer as a Christian" (*ibid.*).

These data are thrown into high relief in the light

[1] Moffatt, *Introduction to the Literature of the New Testament* (New York, 1925), pp. 318–44.

of Pliny's letter. The governor wrote to Trajan because he was in doubt of the proper manner of conducting the trial of Christians. Pending instruction, he has examined several who had been accused by delation. He thrice put to these the question whether they were Christians, the repetition itself including strong sanction to deny the fact. He took it that persistent maintenance of the loyalty was worthy of punishment. A convenient test was the introduction of images of the gods and of the emperor; non-Christians performed approved rites and reviled Christ, but those who were Christians could not be induced to do so. It was learned that the cult was in effect harmless, accompanied by no debasing features. The members were obedient when their meetings were dissolved on the basis of an imperial edict prohibiting societies. Indeed, Pliny thought that the situation might easily be met; there were signs already of the weakening of its influence. Temples were being frequented and victims bought, which had not until the time of writing been true.

The coincidence of the data of Pliny's letter and that ascribed to Peter is extensive. In the first place, it is the major care of the Christian letter that its public be so exemplary in character that if tests come the people shall be found blameless. It is solicitous that the people be law-abiding. It is meticulously careful that due honor shall be done the King. In sort, both generally and in detail I Peter meets the Pliny-Trajan situation.

Second, the letter counsels a mediating policy in political outlook. Its advice is to

submit to all human authority, for the Lord's sake. To the Emperor as supreme, to governors as sent by him to punish wrongdoers but to praise those who do good. For it is God's will that by doing good you shall silence the ignorant charges of senseless men. . . . . Honor all; love the brotherhood; fear God, honor the Emperor [I Pet. 2:13–17].

This is exactly the political attitude urged by Paul, who had a high appreciation of the power of the Roman order (Rom. 13:1–7), and, indeed, is in agreement with the Pharisaic political attitude which was articulated by Jesus in the Gospels (Matt. 22:15–22; Mark 12:13–17; Luke 20:20–26). The attitude is in sharp contrast to that expressed in the Book of Revelation, in which the emperor is called a beast, who is to be resisted, not honored. The exhortation to honor the emperor immediately reminds one of the statement of the Scillitan martyr, who said, "We give honor to Caesar as Caesar, but we render fear to our God." Indeed, this letter is careful to make such a distinction, as it exhorts: "Sanctify in your hearts Christ as Lord" (I Peter 4:7). The attitude toward the state is conservative.

In I Peter, too, Jesus is the great martyr example. His sufferings were predicted in Scripture (4:7), and it is to be expected that his followers shall suffer unjustly also (2:21 ff.). If they suffer unjustly, they must patiently endure. Indeed, to suffer for righteousness is blessedness (3:14 ff.). They should not fear; but, on the other hand, if accused, they should be ready with their defense "if anyone questions you on account of the hope which you have in you." This is to be done respectfully, so that the accusers may be put to shame. It would appear from the letter that their situation was apparent.

Do not be surprised that a fiery test is occurring among you, but be glad that you are in a measure sharing Christ's sufferings. . . . . If you are being tortured in the name of Christ, you are blessed. For no one should suffer as a murderer, a thief, a wrongdoer, or a meddler; but if one suffers as a Christian, he must not be ashamed of it, but must give honor to God in this name [4:12–16].

It may be recalled that Pliny's letter exhibits the desire of the governor to be as lenient with Christians as possible, since no overt evil acts are found to characterize them, but also a willingness, where guilt of being a Christian is persistently confessed, sharply to punish them, since such obstinate unwillingness to conform to approved religions is worthy of punishment. It is in view of this that I Peter's message appears to receive point; its readers are urged, above all, to be guilty of no evil deeds but to be faithful in their willingness to be punished if they are brought to account for being Christians.

One inquires whether the nearly contemporary letters of Ignatius throw light on the attitudes represented by I Peter. It is obvious that there is not in I Peter that morbid anticipation of martyrdom for the sake of its reward which is so characteristic of Ignatius. There is, however, some similarity in

the two sources in the objective use made of the
sufferings of Jesus. The position of Ignatius, probably because of the eagerness of the bishop for
martyrdom, is a more advanced attitude. With this
relative difference recognized, however, there is to
be seen a certain similarity: "Suffer me to be an
imitator of the passion of my God" (Ignatius *To
the Romans* vi. 3). "Unless we choose to die with
him in the same passion, his life is not in us" (*Mag-
nesians* v. 2). "We are of his fruit from his divinely
blessed passion" (*Smyrneans* i. 2). Clearly both
I Peter and the letters of Ignatius represent stages
in the process by which the example of Jesus became a powerful sanction to induce the martyr attitude, I Peter being somewhat more primitive than
Ignatius. But each makes its contribution.

The method of I Peter is exhortation. Its purpose, like later writings, is preparation for suffering. It therefore belongs to the category of control
literature; it does not propose to leave the issue to
chance, but, recognizing the likelihood of suppres-
sive measures, it urges its public to be ready to
meet them. Its highest sanction is the example of
Christ, although reward obtains emphasis. Indeed,
it appears that pleasure may derive from the experience; the sufferer is called blessed, recalling the
Gospel beatitude on persecution. The voluntary
acceptance of martyrdom is assumed throughout.

Thus, while I Peter is not as advanced in certain
respects as other sources of nearly the same date,
it is by no means primitive. Note, for example, its

antithesis of the Gospel recommendation that one's words of confession be left to the inspiration of the moment (Mark 13:11); I Peter not merely urges that one be prepared for his defense (3:15), but it is careful to say that "since Christ suffered in the flesh, arm yourselves with the same mind" (4:1). Charismatic inspiration was apparently the most primitive hope for the induction of the willingness to undergo martyrdom; I Peter is nearer the later point of view in which Christian groups saw to it that candidates were prepared by controllable processes.

It is of course a basic problem, if I Peter is regarded as coming from the time of Trajan, that the work is ascribed to Peter. In other words, the problem is similar to that of the Pastoral Epistles. To be sure, pseudonymity is not itself a problem; it was common enough to be regarded as a mere convention. Particularly it is nothing exceptional that a letter of Trajan's period should be ascribed to Peter, who presumably died in Nero's time, for the apocryphal gospel, acts, letters, and apocalypse published with his name furnish an abundance of parallels. The phenomenon of pseudonymity in an alleged letter of Peter's, whose function was control in a situation of suppression, is readily understood in the light of the process by which Peter was given heroic importance as a proto-martyr, in the same way that he achieved priority as the chief of apostles. The tradition of his martyrdom, current in the Christian version of the Ascension of Isaiah and witnessed in I Clement, made Peter valuable as an apostolic example, and it was this value which made his name useful to a pseudonymous letter whose message concerned the martyr experience. This doubtless explains the letter's reference to its supposed writer as "the . . . . martyr [μάρτυς] of *witness* the sufferings of the Christ" (5:1).

It is fitting, indeed, that such use should be made of Peter's fame; the tradition was clearly available at the time. Ignatius, who hoped ardently to attain similar status, refers to his approaching fate, and requests that no attempt be made to cause its evasion. He goes on to say, "I do not order you as Peter and Paul did . . . ." (*To the Romans* iv. 3). If the two martyr apostles were so readily in the memory of the martyr bishop in Trajan's time, surely Peter's name was useful to a letter designed to meet a critical situation.

The third of the earlier situations of suppression which throws light on early Christian literature was the tension which was apparent during the last years of Domitian. It has been pointed out that it has been denied that Domitian's eccentricities involved any but some of the Roman higher class.[1] However, historians generally take a different view.[2] It appears, indeed, that the situation of strain was felt even by Josephus, and was reflected in his contemporary writing.[3] Christian tradition is

[1] Merrill, *Essays in Early Christian History* (London, 1924), pp. 148–73.

[2] Cf. Linsenmayer, *Die Bekämpfung des Christentums durch den römischen Staat* (München, 1905), pp. 65–84.

[3] Cf. Case, "Josephus' Anticipation of a Domitianic Persecution," *Journal of Biblical Literature*, XLIV (1925), 10–20.

explicit in its statement of such a condition.[1] It appears to have influenced the writing of the New Testament Apocalypse, I Clement, and the Epistle to the Hebrews, and possibly Luke-Acts.[2] Many New Testament scholars, as was noted above, relate I Peter to the period of Domitian. Clearly, such abundant attestation results from a definite situation.

It is a feature of the greatest importance that this situation caused the writing of the apocalyptic type, which, it has been shown, was the normal type of Jewish persecution literature. Are we at a point earlier than Christianity's development of its own literary form of control literature? Is this New Testament Apocalypse, so Jewish in character, an exception to the characteristic development of distinct methods of control?

In answering this question, it must be observed that the Book of Revelation carries at the beginning a series of letters—one general, seven to churches. It is only after the letters that the properly apocalyptic sections occur. This is an important modification of type.

Further, the letters are full of matter which is similar to the typical Christian forms of control writing. First, they aim to control by direct exhortation. Second, the exhortation is always individualistically directed; the reward is always promised "to him who conquers" (Rev. 2:7, 11, 17, 26;

---

[1] Tertullian *Apology* v.

[2] Goodspeed, *The Story of the New Testament* (Chicago, 1916), pp. 75-99.

3:5, 12, 21). Third, the content is typically martyrological. For example, the predictions of suffering,
the exhortations to stedfastness, the urge to be
faithful, the praise to those who did not deny the
name, and so on. Of special significance is the centering of attention to "Antipas my faithful martyr"
(μάρτυς, 2:13). The presence of such details marks
this apocalypse as untypical in these respects.
These are individualistic phenomena, presumably
present because the whole work is to a certain degree modified by forces from its Hellenistic environment.

This leads to the notice that the province of Asia
was the provenance of the letters and presumably of
the work as a whole. Asia was the locality in which
Christianity was earliest firmly integrated into the
gentile world, where gentile Christianity first obtained its character. Here, or at any rate in the
Aegean Basin as a whole, the political apologies had
their rise. In view of such facts, modification in the
direction of Hellenistic environmental forces is to
be expected, even in an apocalypse.

Reference to Asia leads also to the notice that the
first martyr is named as a Pergameme. Now
Pergamum was then the seat of the cult of the emperor. It is significant that the first-named martyr
obtained his distinction where the imperial cult was
most obvious. Asia, it will be remembered, was the
province which first petitioned the emperor that
the cult might be organized. Asia was always enthusiastic in its support, and its cities evinced simi-

lar enthusiasm in organizing municipal organizations of the worship of the emperor. It was but natural that Christians should first become involved with it in Asia.

It was the imperial cult which shaped the messages of the New Testament Apocalypse. It accounts for the emphasis so frequent in the work upon the denial of the Name. Likewise, the later mention of images (Rev. 13:14 f.; 15:2; 19:19; 20:4) probably implies accoutrement of the cult. It is almost explicit when the worship of the beast and the acceptance of the beast's seal are cited as the unspeakable apostasy (13:4, 8, 15, 16 ff.; 19:20; 20:4).

The control task of the work being thus specific, what was its method? Here, again, features not typical of the Palestinian Jewish apocalypses appear. The appeal of John's revelation was so largely to the individual that the usual unit of attention in typical apocalypses, the group, is very much in the background. Such is the case in the usual warning: "If anyone worships the beast and his image, and receives the seal upon his forehead or upon his hand, he shall himself drink of the wine of God's anger" (14:9 f.). Control is here narrowly directed.

Similarly, the individualistic emphasis upon the martyr illustrates the control method. It is clearly untypical of the apocalypse that the martyrs are represented as already in heaven, in anticipation of other dead. But it is so pictured of those who for their refusal to worship the emperor are already in heaven, where they shall reign with Christ for a millennium (20:4–6). It has been shown how this conception figured as one of the sanctions of reward in the later literature. It is certainly a feature which developed as Christianity became at home in the Hellenistic world, for no Jewish apocalypse has any such datum.[1]

The figures by which the martyrs are otherwise suggested further support the generalization. When smoke of the incense represents their prayers, or when their souls are said to be beneath the altar, where, naturally, the blood dripped, the martyrs have been slain "because of God's word and because of the testimony [μαρτύριαν] which they had" (6:9). The "white stole" is their distinctive dress (6:11, 7:9, 13, 14; 22:14). They are before God's throne, where they continually serve, having neither hunger nor thirst nor suffering other discomfort; God shall wipe away their tears (7:13–17). They have won their place because they "conquered . . . . because of the Lamb's blood and the word of their testimony, and they did not love their life unto death" (12:11). The martyrs have decidedly a more heroic place in this Christian apocalypse than is the custom for their prototypes in Jewish literature of the same sort.

Punishment operates as negative sanction in this work in a manner suggesting the later martyrological writings. The language of the letters to the

---

[1] IV Ezra 7:28, which pictures certain undying companions of the Messiah, is not actually an exception.

seven churches is sometimes stern as faults are pointed out. The fate of those who do not have God's seal on their foreheads, by whom apostates are apparently meant, is grievous. Still more explicit is to be the punishment of those who worshiped the beast, who have accepted his mark rather than God's. These, supposedly devotees of the imperial cults, have the awful punishment figured by the seven bowls of anger. The punishment of Rome is indicated with every grewsome detail. Such features, again, suggest the Hellenistic rather than Jewish influences.

Jesus as proto-martyr is given high place as an example. Indeed, there is hardly any other aspect of Jesus suggested. Certainly there is no teaching of Jesus in the book. Of course it is not relevant to demand it, but at all events it is true that the effectiveness of Jesus is as martyr and inspirer of the persecuted. The general letter at the beginning of the book brings a greeting from "Jesus the faithful martyr" ($\mu\acute{\alpha}\rho\tau\upsilon s$). The sufferers are brothers and sharers in the trouble—the kingdom and the stedfastness in Jesus. Jesus is the slain lamb whose worthiness the mighty chorus chants. It is in the lamb's blood that the martyrs' garments are cleansed. The martyrs conquered through the blood of the lamb. Apostates' names were absent from the life-book of the slain lamb. The figure of the lamb's bride is very effective, since her linen is the righteous acts of the saints. But the victor Lamb is pictured, too, the light of the new city, the

occupant of a throne, whom the triumphant martyrs serve. The conquering warrior Jesus is also
celebrated, an avenging soldier whose army, if the
figure of the white robe is consistent, is made of victorious martyrs. It is this warrior who is King of
kings and Lord of lords. Obviously, these conceptions function toward a martyrological purpose.[1]

Nor is it straining exegesis to point out that in the
New Testament Apocalypse martyrdom is a meri-
torious work. Stedfastness is constantly commend-
ed. The sufferers are exhorted to be faithful unto
death. The faithful are praised because they have
undergone much for the Lord's sake, without
wearying; some, indeed, are praised that they did
not deny. Those who have died cry for vengeance;
and it is promised that, although they shall be rewarded, there must be more deaths. Martyrdom is
to be expected in many cases, and therefore preparation must be made.

It is of course not suggested that the recognition
of modifications due to Hellenistic influences re-
moves the New Testament Apocalypse from the
category of apocalyptic literature. Clearly it is to
be studied in the light of Jewish apocalyptic, with
which literary type it is genetically related. But it
is important to observe that by so early a date as the
end of the first century the influence of the martyrological attitude had become important enough to

[1] The martyrological motif in Revelation is also urged by Lohmeyer,
Die Offenbarung des Johannes (*Handbuch zum Neuen Testament*) (Tübingen,
1926).

cause these modifications. The development of methods of control was already so far advanced that the Jewish type of control literature was no longer used unaltered in Christian circles. New methods of control were working changes.

The full fruit of this process is seen as the Apocalypse of Peter and the *Shepherd* of Hermas are compared with the Revelation of John. As has been shown, the Greek conceptions of punishment clearly mark the character of the pseudo-Petrine apocalypse, while Hermas is still less in conformation to the original Jewish type. In all three of these Christian revelations the influence of control in suppression is obvious. The steadily growing Christian literature, in which the later typical attitude toward martyrdom was beginning to appear, was achieving its own means of effecting control.

Domitian's demand to be called "Lord" and "God" apparently produced in Christian writing not only an apocalypse but letters. It is becoming widely recognized that meaning obtains to many of the statements of the Epistle to the Hebrews when they are read in the light of Domitian's suppression. Further, the relation between this letter and that known as I Clement is made understandable in the light of this unhappy event.

The situation attacked by the letter to the Hebrews may be understood when it is remembered that in the generation between Nero and Domitian the growth of such a congregation as that at Rome has been notable. But, as in the third century, be-

fore the purifying fire of Decius' persecution rid the
churches of many merely nominal Christians, in the
number belonging to the group there were not a
few whose faith was only a veneer. Now that difficulty has come of these many have fallen away;
and the church, which should be in a commanding
position of leadership, has to be stimulated to take
its proper place in meeting the situation. It is to
furnish the stimulus that Hebrews was written.

God, says the writer, again has spoken. One must
heed his message, which, given through Jesus, has
been reiterated and confirmed. How may one escape if he neglects so great a salvation? The readers ought, following a great example, hold fast the
confession (ὁμολογία). But it is necessary to check
incipient falling-away. This will be done by constant exhortation. To hold fast is to partake of
Christ. Are not difficulties always found in the
growth of a faith? But Jesus is the great example.
One must, having him in mind, hold fast the confession. Jesus, the example, had shared every trial.
In the days of his life he had faced death with prayers, supplications, weeping and tears, yet with a
son's obedience. He learned obedience in his suffering, and thus became the author of a faith.

The writer's message was offered with misgiving,
since his readers are dull. The group whose former
glory was such that it ought to be a teacher of
others itself was in need of instruction! Yet teaching was attempted. The group is warned that falling-away is not forgivable, since it amounts to the

recrucifixion of Jesus. The writer hopes that his readers will keep the faith, consequently he exhorts them to imitate them who through faith and stedfastness inherit the promises, of whom Jesus was forerunner—Jesus, the High Priest whose blood offering was none other victim than himself. His covenant is thus new and superior—not so new that it is bloodless—but the blood is Christ's, the testament Christ's death, the holy place heaven. His followers may thus enter that holy place, and are exhorted to do so. But they must hold fast the confession of the hope and not let it waver. They ought to emulate each other in good works, not abandoning the fellowship of the congregation. Again, they are solemnly warned that falling-away cannot be forgiven but will surely be punished.

Perhaps examples may be helpful; the heroes from Abel to the present exhibit the worth of suffering, especially since these suffered without the realization of the reward. Most of all, Jesus is to be noted—the author and perfecter of the faith, who joyfully endured the cross, despising shame, and thus gained the reward. There is, moreover, the entire company of martyrs ($\mu\alpha\rho\tau\acute{\upsilon}\rho\omega\nu$) to incite all with stedfastness to run the course which is set. After all, no one has yet been forced to resist unto blood; such suffering as has occurred is like a parent's chastening. It will result in gain if persistence is maintained. The integrity of the group must be kept; there may be not the least defilement.

A section of practical matter contains a reiteration of the urge to imitate the faith of the former teachers. The sufferings of Jesus are again cited, and the work closes with a prayer for peace and a good issue of the situation.

It should hardly need to be mentioned that these martyrological data are not of an advanced status. Hebrews' contribution to the materials of control is of a less typical or decisive character than is true of those of later dates, when greater familiarity with situations of like nature led to the production of typical forms. Too, the lesser severity of its situation may account for the character of its materials.

But the contribution of Hebrews is not inconsiderable. Observe, for example, its emphasis upon the imitation of former examples. "We desire that each one of you may show the same diligence to the fulness of hope to the very end, that you may be . . . . imitators" (Heb. 6:12). "Remember them who had rule . . . . who spoke God's word, and, considering the issue of their life, imitate their faith" (12:7). The conception is basic to Hebrews and appears to be that which is trusted to win the desired issue.

Now, imitation of heroic examples was not only an important part of the fully worked-out technique of control, but it is a method which is to be found in works reflecting earlier situations. Note the contemporary I Clement: "Let us also be imitators of those who went about 'in the skins of goats and sheep' heralding the coming of Christ"—following which is a list of examples similar to those of Hebrews, chapter 11 (I Clem. 17:1). The martyrdom of Polycarp, the story says, is one which "all desire to imitate" (*Martyrdom of Polycarp* xix. 1). Even more specifically in I Clement the noble examples of Peter and Paul are powerfully urged, "To cease from examples of old time, let us come to those who contended in the days nearest us; let us take the examples of our own generation . . . . Peter . . . . and Paul . . . . the greatest example of endurance" (I Clem. 5). Later use of the sanction has been abundantly cited.

A second phenomenon in Hebrews is the use of the terminology of confession which approaches the later technical usage. Jesus is the apostle and high priest of our confession (Heb. 3:1). The readers are urged to "hold fast the confession" (4:14; 10:23). The final exhortation is specially representative: "Jesus . . . . suffered death. . . . . Let us go out to him . . . . sharing the contempt which he endured. . . . . Let us in his name offer praise as a sacrifice to God, that is fruit of lips confessing his name" (13:15).

But doubtless the point at which Hebrews approaches type is its use of Jesus as martyr. This value is found throughout the book. It is early said (Heb. 2:10 f.) that Jesus was crowned with glory and honor through suffering death, and this is explained as proper that God thus made Jesus a leader who was qualified through what he suffered. Jesus' sharing of human temptation resulted in his triumphant death, since he learned obedience through suffering. He thus became the author of salvation. Jesus is a forerunner of the hope which lay before the readers (6:20). His suffering was endured so that he might consecrate the people through his own blood. But, of course, it is the citation of Jesus at the end of the long line of heroes which makes the climax: they are the crowd of heavenly martyrs, in the sight of whom the readers are to enter the contest, fixing their gaze upon Jesus the leader and perfecter of faith, who accepted the cross and has been elevated to share God's throne (12:1 f.).

Surely the purpose to which the series of examples, with Jesus as chief, is directed becomes eloquent when it is seen in the light of Domitian's suppression.

Consider him who endured such gainsaying . . . . that you do not become weary, fainting in your souls. You have not yet resisted unto blood in striving against sin; you have forgotten the exhortation which reasons with you as sons. . . . . It is for chastening that you endure; God is dealing with you as sons. . . . . For they did indeed for a few days chasten us as seemed good to them. . . . . All chastening seems for the present to be grievous, not joyous, yet afterward peaceable fruit is yielded to them who have been exercised by it. . . . . Therefore lift up the hands that hang down, and the palsied knees, and make straight paths for your feet, so that the lame may not be diverted, but rather be healed [Heb. 12:3–13].

If this is the writer's reference to the suppression of Domitian, it would appear that the situation was less severe than that of the public of Revelation.

This estimate would agree with the hypothesis that the letter had Rome for its destination; it is probable that Domitian's bid for deification had much less severe consequence in Rome than in Asia. Or, the lesser severity may be accounted for by the period in the situation when the letter was written; if, as is supposed, Hebrews preceded I Clement, it is understandable on this basis why the latter pictures a more severe suppression. First Clement is a reflection of events which were later than the background of Hebrews.

However this may be, the writer's purpose is evident. The group to whom his letter was directed was shaken by the action taken against it. There were wavering, indecision, and apostasy. They, who by virtue of their position ought to be leaders, were as babes who needed instruction in the rudiments. When another such situation had occurred (Heb. 10:32–39), they had been models of stedfastness. Certainly such faithfulness ought now to obtain, and to this end the writer attacks the problem of control.

According to an interesting hypothesis, Hebrews' exhortation to the Roman church succeeded in stinging this group into action. They proceeded to meet their untoward situation, apparently undergoing much suffering in consequence. Having attained something like creditable status, a leader of the church in effect wrote a reply to the Epistle to the Hebrews. The so-called First Letter of Clement to the Corinthians thus becomes an additional witness to the ways in which Christians met the problems of the suppression of Domitian.

It was this unhappy event, presumably, that the writer has in mind when he refers to the "sudden and repeated misfortunes which have befallen us" (I Clem. 1:1). Whether the sufferings of certain persons mentioned later were of the same case, it is impossible to say. At any rate there is reference to "a great multitude . . . . who were the victims of jealousy and offered amongst us the fairest example in their endurance under many indignities and tortures" (6:1). "We are in the same arena, and the same struggle is before us" (7:1).

First Clement attacks his problem of control much as the Epistle to the Hebrews does. He cites a list of examples of stedfastness, beginning, as Hebrews does, with Abel, and ending with "those who contended in the days nearest us . . . . the noble examples of our own generation" (5:1). The sufferings of Peter and Paul are the norm, since these were persecuted and contended unto death. It is urged that their experiences be before the eyes of the readers. Peter suffered not few, but many, trials; Paul suffered often and gave his testimony (μαρτυρήσας) before the rulers (chap. 5).

The language of the letter is quite comparable to that of typical martyrological literature. The martyrs are called "athletes," a figure often used in the martyrologies. There is purposeful utilization of the sanction of reward. Paul, for example, "was taken up into the Holy Place" (5:7); Peter "went to the glorious place which was his due" (5:4); and the larger group of lesser heroes "received a noble reward" (6:3). The examples are cited for the control purpose; "Let us fix our eyes upon the good apostles" (5:3). Paul "showed the way to the prize of stedfastness" (5:5) and is thus "the greatest example of stedfastness" (5:7). Of course, most appealing of sanctions was the proto-martyr: "Let us fix our gaze upon the blood of Christ" (7:4).

First Clement may be cited as a corroborating witness of the suppression of Domitian. Like Hebrews, it is of the letter form rather than apocalyptic. Also like Hebrews, it approaches rather than realizes the typical development of method in meeting its situation. It is thus instructive as illustrating the growth of technique more than its habituated application. These sources are the sort which is to be expected in an earlier situation.

It may be suggested, finally, that the messages of Luke-Acts, the Gospel and the second volume to Theophilus, in part took their shape by reason of the strained situation of Domitian's suppression. Their provenance was probably the Aegean Basin, where the action was most felt. A major purpose of the double work, as has long since been recognized, was to show the political innocuousness of Christianity.[1] This appears most plainly in Acts, where pains are taken to point out how a Roman court had dismissed a complaint against a leader of the new faith (Acts 18:12–17). The reviews of Paul's

[1] Moffatt, *op. cit.*, pp. 303 f.

case after his arrest skilfully suggest his innocence. Recently Professor Cadbury has pointed out that the language of Luke's preface may be taken as implying the purpose of correcting the wrong impression of the new movement gained by a Roman official.[1] These data, and others which are relevant, when regarded in conjunction with the weighty literary reasons for dating Luke-Acts about 95, become even more significant when considered in the light of Domitian's suppression.[2]

If these suggestions are correctly based, it follows that the influence of persecution or like activity is to be traced into the periods of the composition of the New Testament. It is not to be expected that in so early a time the problems presented by coercive activity were solved, or that such a body of method and materials was available that later periods possessed. But to observe the growth of these methods and materials is no less instructive than to see their application. The relatively abundant reflection of the earlier situations in literature enables the observation of evolving attitudes and gradually developed techniques. The processes are immensely instructive, in earlier as in later situations, for their contributions in social control.

[1] Cadbury, "The Purpose Expressed in Luke's Preface," *The Expositor*, VIII, No. 31 (1921), 431–41.

[2] Riddle, *Jesus and the Pharisees* (Chicago, 1928), pp. 149 f., "The Occasion of Luke-Acts" *Journal of Religion*, X (1930), 545–62.

VIII

A PRIMITIVE MARTYROLOGY

It was a trying fact for the early Christians that certain earlier situations which shared the nature of persecutions had to be faced before techniques for meeting them were available. The fact makes even more instructive such evidence of evolving method as is furnished by the New Testament and other early literature. It may be affirmed that there is no more striking or instructive example than that primitive martyrology, the Gospel according to Mark, which a growing consensus places in Rome at about A.D. 70.[1]

Nero figures largely in Christian tradition as a persecutor. To be sure, there is doubt that there was a Neronic persecution;[2] but it may be suggested that, when it is recognized that the action described by Tacitus[3] and mentioned by Suetonius[4] was not a true persecution, but a punishment of Christians on other than religious ground, the force of the Christian tradition may be fairly understood. Obviously, there was no general action taken against the Christians as such. But apparently Tacitus is to be followed when he refers to Nero's skilful shifting of

[1] Bacon, *Is Mark a Roman Gospel?* (Cambridge, 1919).

[2] Arnold, *Die Neronische Christenverfolgung; eine kritische Untersuchung zur Geschichte der ältesten Kirche* (Leipzig, 1888).

[3] *Annals* xv. 44.   [4] *Nero* 16.

suspicion to Christians and then causing their punishment for the crime of arson.

At all events, Nero made a deep impression upon Christian tradition. Not only do the later writers identify him as the first of the persecutors,[1] but earlier references are available. Mention may be made of the Sybilline Oracles; as early as this the myth of Nero's reappearance was familiar. But in Christian sources the impress of Nero upon the work called the Ascension of Isaiah is of greater interest. Here the identification of the Emperor is hardly veiled; he is the murderer of his mother, who is to persecute the plant planted by the twelve apostles of the Well Beloved, into whose hands one of the twelve shall fall. Further, the *redivivus* myth, his miracles, and his demand for worship add to the significance of this witness of a martyrological work (4:1 ff.).

Still earlier there is apparently a Neronic source in the Johannine apocalypse. At all events, such is the usual interpretation of the head of the beast which, after receiving a mortal wound, revives (13:3)—the Nero-*redivivus* myth. There is some agreement, too, that the famous cryptogram (13: 18) is the seer's guarded reference to Nero. This name is suggested as the solution of the number in two significant studies of Revelation.[2]

It is important to observe what is indicated by

---

[1] Melito in Eusebius *HE* iv. 26. 9; Tertullian *Apology* 5.

[2] Case, *The Revelation of John* (Chicago, 1919), pp. 310 ff.; Charles, *International Critical Commentary*, "Revelation" (New York, 1920), I, 364 ff.

the Neronic source in the Apocalypse. Not only does it witness to the common expectation that the dead Emperor would reappear, but it envisages his reappearance in a highly portentous manner. He will perform notable wonders, and these will lead many astray. He will be worshiped, and those who do not render this homage will be grievously punished. The beast's war with the saints is proleptically pictured; the beast was strong enough to triumph, so that the expected fate is that those destined for captivity shall be seized and those for the sword shall die; on this certainty rest the patient endurance and fidelity of the saints. Jesus is not absent from the seer's mind; he is called the slain lamb (13:8).

It is doubtful to what extent one should personify the second beast of the Neronic source. It is doubtless correct to take the figure as suggesting a priest of the imperial cult; the references to the demand for worship are otherwise meaningless. If this meaning is correct, the function of the cult of the Emperor in the time of the writing of the source, or perhaps the time of its incorporation into the Apocalypse, is important for the writer's outlook and purpose. It gives point to his expectation of slaughter and to his daring resistance to the demand that his fellows receive the imperial seal and offer the usual homage.

It is thus apparent that whatever must be one's judgment concerning a Neronic "persecution," Nero figured importantly in Christian tradition which was concerned with the control task.

There arises an arresting question. According to an increasing consensus the Gospel according to Mark had its rise in Rome about the year 70. Does the earliest gospel exhibit any influence of the strained emotions so common to the early Christians by reason of their fear and apprehension of Nero?

The question is forced not only by reason of the book's writing at the time and in the place where Nero was an ominous figure, but by reason of the content of the earliest gospel. It has long been noticed, and the fact recognized as a problem of first importance, that the Markan gospel devotes some half its meager space to a relation of events leading up to and describing Jesus' passion, and that in these materials there is a utilization of the apocalyptic method which is essentially primitive. These factors, it is believed, assume specific character when the Gospel according to Mark is studied in the light of the early Christian expectation of martyrdom.

Consider the circumstances in which the work had its rise. In the year 64 occurred the burning of Rome. Whether or no the fire was set by Nero, it became the cause of the Emperor's mistreatment of a number of Christians, whose sufferings were cited not only in later tradition but in earlier works. Their fortitude wins praise in the letter to the Hebrews (10:32–34). Not only the unnamed lesser heroes are figuratively mentioned in Clement's letter to Corinth, but thus early appears the tradition of the martyrdom of Peter and Paul (I Clem. 5).

In 66 began the war in Palestine, which in 70 ended with the Holy City laid waste and the Temple in ruins. What did these terrible events portend?

Surely such a sequence would justify an expression of the apocalyptic prediction. To any who thought in such terms the end of the age might have seemed imminent. What would have been more likely to have precipitated into writing a work which offers a program for the past and the immediate future? What can be suggested better to account for the purpose and content of the Gospel according to Mark?

To be sure, some elements of this hypothetical situation are speculative. Chief of these are the traditions of the deaths of Peter and Paul. It is recognized that uncertainty attends these traditions at many points. However, recent investigation[1] justifies confidence that Rome's possession of her most valued "trophies" may go back to the martyrdoms, which at all events have been effective as martyrological data.

It is in the Gospel itself that are found the reasons for reading it in the light of the Neronic situation. It is in connection with these factors that the criteria which have been developed may be applied. Confidence results from their application. What, for example, was the purpose of Mark's recounting

[1] Lietzmann, *Petrus und Paulus in Rom. Liturgische und archäeologische Studien* (Berlin und Leipzig, 1927). Cf. La Piana, "The Tombs of Peter and Paul ad Catacumbas," *Harvard Theological Review*, XIV (1921), 53-94, and Lietzmann, "The Tomb of the Apostles ad Catacumbas," *ibid.*, XVI (1923), 147-62.

at such length and in such detail the story of Jesus' death? Was it not to furnish the supreme example of the fortitude with which his followers should hope to meet death? To be sure, even Paul made much of "the word of the cross." But it is Mark who gave the story definitive form. Oral tradition presumably was various, but in this early gospel there is a fixed form which became normative for later narrations. Mark thus not only is important as fixing its form, but more so in its immense influence upon subsequent literature. It is highly significant that in the Markan plan of materials the passion and resurrection story occupy more than half the total bulk of the work. This was not accidental. At any rate, the later gospels, with more of a didactic interest, alter the proportion. Mark intended the passion story to be the most important element in his gospel.

The climax of the Markan gospel is, as in the Greek tragedy, in the recognition scene of chapter 8. Jesus, who before was adequately recognized only by abnormal beings, is shown to be God's Anointed. But the significant point is the particular kind of Anointed. Jesus is to be one who suffers and dies. Consequently the theme of the falling action of Mark is not Jesus as Messiah, but Jesus whose way is the way of the Cross. Immediately after his recognition Jesus makes the first of the three announcements of his death (8:31), and, moreover, assures his followers that a like fate awaits them and that they must surely accept it (8:34 f.). Reward for acceptance, or punishment for failure, is suggested.

The suffering Anointed is given still more certain recognition in a scene where Peter, James, and John are privileged to witness Jesus talk about his impending martyrdom with Moses and Elias (9: 2–8). Subsequent discussion introduces dogmatic ground and Scriptural sanction to make the martyrdom believable. Indeed, by ingenious identification John's death is made a proto-martyrdom.

Before the group turn toward Jerusalem, further preparation is given in the second prediction of Jesus' death (9:31). And again, with keen subtlety it is suggested that suffering is in store for his followers. For the story is told of one who was unable to follow, who is made the example for the teaching that discipleship entails sacrifice and suffering, even persecution (10:29). But to those who accept their fate, there is promised rich reward (10:30).

Now Mark pictures Jesus and his company on the way to Jerusalem. There is something ominous about the fact; the disciples are afraid. Consequently Jesus imparts (for the third time in Mark's plan) the intelligence of his death. Obviously, purpose is served by the reiteration.

Immediately in connection Mark relates a heroic story. James and John request positions of eminence in the coming Kingdom, and base the propriety of their request upon their readiness, which they boldly affirm, to "drink the cup" which Jesus is to drink, and to "be baptized" with his baptism.

These figures obtain meaning in the light of the passion story; in effect the two brothers state their willingness to suffer and die. What is the purpose of this story? It is well known that James in an early tradition was a martyr; there is also tradition to the effect that John suffered the martyr's death. To be sure, the story about John is not excellently attested.[1] It may be said, whatever the statement is worth, that this story is one, perhaps the strongest, link in the elevation of James and John to the dignity of martyrs. The story thus contributes to the martyr *motif* in the Markan gospel.

The rapidly moving passion story presently brings Jesus into Jerusalem, and, of course, into the conflict which precipitates his fate. He exercises his authority, which already has been pictured as extending over nature, to challenge the Temple group, with the result that his death is sought. Challenge is carried into debate, the climax of which appears in the story by which a meaningful murder pictures the rejection of the "stone of stumbling," which became the cornerstone of a new structure. A play of wits clarifies for Mark's readers Jesus' attitude toward the state.

In the passion story the longest section of sustained didactic contains an apocalyptic message. In it the entire cosmic program is foretold. It includes, not merely pseudo-messiahs, but wars, rumors of wars, and, significantly, persecutions.

[1] Cf. Moffatt, *Introduction to the Literature of the New Testament* (New York, 1925), pp. 602 ff.

Jesus' followers, it is predicted, shall be delivered to sanhedrins, beaten in synagogues, and forced to witness before governors and kings, all on account of Jesus. In such situations one was not to depend upon forethought; inspiration would be sufficient. Indeed, it would be not himself but the Holy Spirit which filled him who would answer the questions. It was an evil situation which is foreseen: one would be betrayed by his brother, a father denounces his child, and children cause the death of their parents. Everyone shall hate the disciple for the Name's sake, but stedfastness shall win salvation.

Obviously, to regard these sayings in the light of the known experiences of the early Christians is immensely instructive. One is reminded of I Clement's references to Peter who "suffered not only one or two but many trials, and having thus given his testimony went to the glorious place which was his due," and to Paul who "taught righteousness to all the world . . . . , gave his testimony before the rulers . . . . passed from the world and was taken up into the holy place—the greatest example of endurance." But even more significant is the advice against forethought and the dependence upon inspiration. It is clear that the leaders presently substituted preparation for inspiration. Mark thus represents a relatively primitive method of inducing the confession. It is, in effect, in close agreement with the Pauline evaluation of charismata (I Cor. 12–14).

The apocalyptic message is followed by the story of the plot of Judas and the priests, whereupon the final elements of the drama quickly unfold. At the Last Supper the note of the vicarious death of Jesus is saddened by the consciousness of his betrayal. Woe to the betrayer! One of the disciple band! Better, indeed, had he never been born. But Jesus thoughtfully warns the company that all will be scandalized. Peter interjects that, though all others might, yet not he; but Jesus predicts Peter's denial (the term is ἀπαρνέομαι, as in the typical martyrological literature). All agree that not even death would cause them to deny.

The agony in the garden, at which Peter, James, and John (the three apostolic martyrs?) were the chosen company is probably that to which Hebrews refers in stating that Jesus was tempted in all points as his followers were. Jesus prays that his cup be removed, and the hour pass away from him, but resigns himself to his Father's will. Peter, who has recently been warned of his denial, is counseled to watch and pray lest he enter into temptation, for though the spirit may be willing the flesh is weak.

The story of betrayal and arrest is chronicled in a manner which exhibits reflection and purpose; it is insisted that what occurred was in fulfilment of the writings. Even in the primitive martyrology, the influence of Old Testament example was strong.

The stories of the legal proceedings carry several interests. In the trial before the Jewish authorities the figure of Peter appears in close association with Jesus. The innocence of Jesus is plainly shown, and his straightforward affirmation in response to the high priest's question contrasts painfully with Peter's denial, which, predicted before, now has its sorry chronicle. Pilate saw that Jesus was delivered up because of envy; he would have preferred to release him, but deferred to the demand of the mob.

Jesus' punishment began immediately, and with short but graphic touches the narrative records the crucifixion. This terrible story is related without the touches of relief which the later evangelists give it. Even so, Mark notes that above the head of the crucified was the legend "The King of the Jews"; shows that the death was accompanied by marvels; and cites the officer's confession, "Certainly this man was a son of God!" The story of the passion is followed by the narratives of the burial and resurrection, where the Gospel apparently is broken in the middle of a sentence.

Even so brief a recapitulation of the salient features of the Markan passion story reveals some of the items which have been found to function in the fully developed martyrologies. First in importance is the exhibition in graphic detail of the exemplary sufferings of Jesus. In the martyrological works, including some contained in the New Testament as well as the more typical, the example of Jesus constituted one of the strongest of all urges to undertake the experience of martyrdom. That the line of martyrs included not only later heroes,

bishops, apostles, but Jesus himself was the supreme appeal.

It is most significant that Mark's passion story
set a type which was closely followed. The significance appears when it is remembered how notable
martyrdoms were recognized to be "according to
the gospel," so that literary parallels might be cited.
The suggestion, of which much use was made, that
Jesus accompanied the martyr in his experience,
and actually suffered with him, came ultimately
from the story of Jesus' passion which thus functioned as a primitive martyrology.

There are other features. The specific interest in
other martyrs may be mentioned. Such is the point
of the stories which single out for special place
James, Peter, and John; the story of the boldness
of the two brothers, and the story of Peter's denial,
which had its full significance in the light of its un-
recorded sequel. There is the use of sanctions which
are perfectly familiar in later martyrologies: predictive prophecy, Scripture fulfilment, and reward
or punishment. Of great importance is the matter
of the behavior of the individual under examination. While the Markan gospel urges dependence
upon charismatic inspiration, whereas the typical
martyrologies utilize specific indoctrination, both
recognize the cruciality of the moment of confession.

It is well to note further the primitivity of this
basic aspect of the primitive martyrology. One of
the distinctive features of the Markan passion story

is the inclusion of the reference to a recommended type of behavior at the moment of confession. The teaching which depends upon charismatic inspiration is contained in an apocalyptic discourse. This itself is an unusual characteristic. As has been shown, the martyrology had its rise and development quite apart from the apocalyptic literary type; the two represent different methods of dealing with the situations of persecution. But in Mark the two aspects appear together. This suggests that the martyrological character of the passion story is indeed primitive, since it represents a stage before the two methods were differentiated. The primitive martyrology is partly inclusive of primitive apocalyptic.

The apocalyptic discourse of Mark, chapter 13, paralleled in Matthew, chapter 24, and Luke, chapter 21, has been the subject of much discussion. It has been noticed that it represents a literary source for the earliest gospel[1] ("let him who reads understand" [vs. 14]), a source which must have had its rise in the portentous events culminating in the destruction of the Temple and of Jerusalem. The arresting suggestion was made by Colani[2] that this little apocalypse may be that "revelation" mentioned by Eusebius in his recital of the story of those days. Eusebius states, it will be remembered, that when the siege was clearly imminent the Chris-

[1] Moffatt, *op. cit.*, pp. 207 ff.

[2] Colani, *Jésus-Christ et les croyances messianiques de son temps* (Strasbourg, 1864), pp. 201 ff.

tians living in Jerusalem abandoned the city and withdrew to Pella, doing so at the direction of "a divine revelation given to men of approved piety before the war" (*Church History* iii. 5. 2). Colani's identification of Mark, chapter 13, as this revelation is largely followed.

It may then be concluded that the earliest evangelist incorporated a primitive apocalypse into his story of Jesus' martyrdom, thus utilizing both the methods of apocalyptic and of martyrology. In other words, this practical martyrology is found to be primitive in that it does not follow one method of control to the exclusion of another.

It has been shown that developed experience in dealing with situations of persecution resulted in the distinction of the apocalyptic from the martyrological method. The apocalypse was found to be typical of, and localized in, Palestinian Judaism, while the martyrology became the characteristic method of dealing with situations of persecution in Hellenistic lands. Thus, not only the Christian martyrologies of the fully developed type belong to the stream of Hellenistic influence, but the Jewish books of II and IV Maccabees exhibit the characteristics of that control literature which is at home in the West. The typically Jewish apocalypses, on the other hand, differently direct their attempt to control. It is the individual who is the unit of control in the martyrological literature, while the apocalypse directs its attention to the preservation of the group by appealing to the group.

It was shown that the apocalyptic method fell into disuse in Christianity as Christianity adapted itself to the Graeco-Roman world. Indeed, those so-called "apocalypses," the Shepherd of Hermas and the Revelation of Peter, were found to be by no means true to type; and the New Testament apocalypse, the Revelation of John, exhibits obvious modifications which reveal the influence of Hellenistic thought.

It is therefore highly interesting that the earliest gospel incorporated a little apocalypse in its martyrological passion story. It is all the more interesting when it is observed that this apocalypse does not exhibit any signs of such modification as marked the Johannine revelation as not strictly true to type. The primitive martyrology contains a primitive apocalypse. It may be called "primitive" because it does not depart from type. It is untinctured by individualism. In it the group is the unit to which control is directed.

Of course the Markan apocalypse in other respects is normal. It cites the usual series of portents. There are the messianic woes and the messianic consummation. There are pseudo-messiahs, corrupted believers, wars, famines, and earthquakes. There are those fearful phenomena of nature, a darkened sun, a dimmed moon, falling stars, and shaken heavenly powers. Only after these signs comes the Son of Man. These data are elemental in the apocalypses.

For the present purpose the essential feature of

this apocalypse is that messianic woe in which persecution figures, when brother shall deliver up
brother, father shall denounce son, and children
shall cause the death of parents. The company of
believers shall be universally hated. They are
therefore exhorted; he who is stedfast shall be redeemed. Now, it is interesting, and indubitably
significant, that only once is the exhortation
phrased in the singular number. The unit elsewhere
is the group. It is the group who are to be delivered
to councils and beaten in synagogues. It is the
group who must stand before kings and governors.
The direction to depend upon inspiration at the
moment of confession is addressed to the group; it
is not they, but the Holy Spirit, who shall speak.

It is exactly at this point that the later examples
of Christian apocalypses modify the true apocalyptic type. They are characterized by traces of individualism. They direct their method of control to
the individual. But the Markan apocalypse has the
group for its unit of control. Its object is the maintenance of the integrity of the group, not the training of the individual for martyrdom.

Of course the function of the passion story as a
primitive martyrology was inclusive of this purpose. The Markan gospel secured its end by using
together two methods of control which in later development were sharply separated. Whereas fully
developed martyrologies are non-apocalyptic, the
primitive martyrology included both non-apocalyptic and apocalyptic materials. It used the apoc-

alypse as an appeal to the group, and the passion story as a whole to appeal to the individual.

It is not suggested that the Gospel according to Mark is a martyrology. To be sure, more than half the bulk of its materials is contained in the section whose major interest is Jesus' death. But Mark is of course a gospel. It is much more than a martyrology. Nevertheless, it is important to recognize the martyrological character of its passion story. It is not too much to call it a primitive martyrology.

It is no new assertion that the "persecution" of Nero and the writing of the Gospel according to Mark were not merely contemporary but related phenomena. It is here urged that the significance of the relation is much greater when the earliest gospel is viewed in the light of the literature of martyrdom. The work had a message which assumes definiteness when the series of calamities of Nero's reign are taken into account. An untoward suppression of a religious group, the death of one and another chief leader, a war ending in slaughter and desolation—perhaps some of Mark's readers saw the triumph of Titus—might very probably cause the writing of a work which was designed to guide the perplexed.

Such is thought to be a justifiable inference since known facts demonstrate that similar situations produced somewhat comparable literature. The phenomena of the Neronic suppression are understandable since they resemble later and better-known practices. Nero's action was one of those which found the Christians less well prepared for trouble than was true at later dates. This explains why the primitive martyrology does not at points conform to type. It should not be expected so to conform. It valuably assisted in making the type. For later situations, from which perfectly normal martyrologies came, found heroes who were well enough prepared by exhortation and example so that their martyrdoms might be said to be "according to the Gospel." It was the Gospel, and most particularly the passion story, which furnished the norm.

The primitive martyrology thus exhibits characteristics which were peculiar to it. It depends in certain details upon methods which later works rejected. Yet it may be asserted that the passion story in the Gospel according to Mark, a work born of persecution, is the earliest known example of literary type which became the martyrology. It stands near the beginning of the processes in which apocalyptic was transformed into martyrology. The Markan passion story is the primitive martyrology.

IX

THE MARTYR INTEREST IN THE GOSPELS

It has been suggested that the coercive activity of certain Roman emperors influenced the form of the gospels. Apprehension of what the future held caused the evangelist of the Gospel according to Mark to shape his materials in such a manner that the passion story functioned as a primitive martyrology. The strain so evident in the late days of Domitian is to be observed not only in the Apocalypse, Hebrews, and I Clement. It made it desirable for the author of Luke-Acts, in exhibiting the political innocence of the Christian movement and in pointing out the propriety of its world-wide extension, to approximate the form of the well-known apology[1] in his two-volume address to the official, Theophilus.

But detailed examination demands the recognition that coercive activity not only influenced the form but affected the content of the gospels. As has been pointed out, it was the martyr interest in the gospels which led to the inclusion of the telling example furnished by Peter's denial. It likewise caused the celebration by special citation of such heroes as James, who was early known as a martyr; Peter, even more famous as bishop and martyr; and

[1] Riddle, *Jesus and the Pharisees* (Chicago, 1928), pp. 145 ff.

198

John, who, though the tradition is dubious, achieved in certain circles the same dignity. The figure of Paul in Acts was powerfully exemplary, as his confession was not only made but repeated. That central problem in persecution, the securing of a confession, was met in the earliest gospel, though the method there recommended differs from those developed in later experiences.

These exhibits do not exhaust the number, nor do they suggest the significance, of the data in the Gospels where the martyr interest is found. In Mark, it is true, the martyr interest is apparent only in the materials included in the passion story. The cases cited above, so far as they are Markan, are thus grouped. But as one reads the gospels it becomes apparent that, while Mark was a source of later writings, these contain materials which are not to be found in the Markan source. The martyr interest is to be found both in Matthew and Luke, where they have used Mark as a source and in sections where the earliest gospel was not so used.

Observe, for example, what was done with the saying on persecution in Mark's "Little Apocalypse." There it reads as follows:

But take heed to yourselves. For they shall deliver you up to councils, and you shall be beaten in synagogues; you shall stand before governors and kings for my sake, as a witness [εἰς μαρτύριαν] to them. . . . . But when they are taking you, delivering you up, do not give forethought of what you shall say, but say that which is given you in that very moment; it is not you speaking, but the Holy Spirit. Brother shall deliver up brother to death, a father his child; children shall rise up against parents and shall kill them. You shall be hated by all because of my name. But he who is stedfast to the end, this one shall be delivered [13:9–13].

Now, Matthew and Luke have, at points which closely correspond with Mark's outline, discourses on last things which also agree closely with Mark's discourse in content. When the point under discussion is reached, Matthew summarizes, as follows:

Then they shall deliver you up to affliction, and they shall kill you, and you shall be hated by all nations on account of my name. Many shall then be led astray; they shall deliver one another up and shall hate each other. . . . . But he who is stedfast to the end, this one shall be delivered [24:9–13].

Luke causes Jesus to say this:

They shall lay hands upon you and persecute [διώξουσιν] you, delivering you up to the synagogues and prisons, bringing you before kings and governors on account of my name. It shall turn out to you as a witness. Set it, then, in your minds not to prepare your defense, for I shall give you speech and wisdom such as none of your opponents shall be able to stand against or contradict. You will be delivered up by parents, brothers, kinsmen, and friends, and they will put some of you to death, and you shall be hated by all because of my name. . . . . It is by your stedfastness that you shall win your lives [21:12–19].

It is worthy of note that Matthew and Luke, using Mark as a source, closely follow the discourse on last things in parallel contexts. It is significant that the later gospels follow the earlier in recommending charismatic inspiration as the proper

method upon which dependence is placed in securing the confession.

It is quite essential to observe also that other use
is made of these sayings in the later gospels. Matthew, it should be noticed, compiles one of his five
great discourses upon the subject of the missionary
activity of the twelve apostles. The evangelist
causes Jesus to include in his preparatory teaching
some words upon the troubles facing the missionaries. They are sent out like sheep in the midst of
wolves. Therefore they are told to

beware of men, for they shall deliver you up to councils, and
they shall scourge you in their synagogues; indeed, you shall
be brought before governors and kings on account of me, for a
witness [μαρτύριαν] to them and to the nations. But when they
deliver you up, do not be anxious how or what you shall say,
for in that moment it shall be given you what you shall say.
For it is not you who speak, but your Father's spirit which
speaks in you. Brother shall deliver brother up to death, the
father his child; children shall rise up against parents and kill
them, and you shall be hated by all people because of my
name. But he who is stedfast to the end, that one shall be
delivered [10:17–22].

Matthew adds, "When they persecute [διώκωσιν]
you in this city, flee to the next" (10:23).

Further sayings in the same discourse involve the
martyr interest. The missionaries are warned of a
fate similar to that of Jesus (Matt. 10:24–25) and
are exhorted not to be afraid of people who are
able to kill them, since God who knows of a sparrow's death will look after them. Then Matthew

causes Jesus to enunciate the famous saying about confession and denial: "Everyone who shall confess [ὁμολογήσει] in me before men I in turn shall confess in him before my heavenly Father. But whoever shall deny [ἀρνήσηται] me before men I in turn shall deny him before my heavenly father" (10:32 f.).

It is striking that the terminology which was found in the later martyrological literature as technical is present in the gospels. It is surely not too much to say that what is envisaged by this saying is related to the persecutory activity which later presented church leaders with problems of control. Evidently that problem faced the publics of the gospels and had to be met by the leaders who exerted control in their situations.

For the Matthean discourse goes on to state that one is not to suppose that Jesus came to cast peace upon the earth. His coming caused the appearance of the sword. Families were expected to become broken, and only those who valued their allegiance to Jesus above all other relationships might be counted worthy. Only he who took his cross was worthy; he must lose his life to find it, but in losing his life on account of Jesus he should indeed discover life (10:34–39). These sayings clearly reveal the presence of the martyr interest in representative discourse matter of the Gospel according to Matthew.

As has been shown, Luke also parallels Mark's references to persecution as they stand in the similar reports of Jesus' discourse on last things. But he, as does Matthew, has them in doublet form in a different context. Whereas Matthew includes the martyr interest in the sayings about missionary work, Luke connects the interests with an immediate cause. The Lukan report attaches the sayings to Jesus' rebuke of the (Pharisees and) lawyers; according to Luke, Jesus predicts that these opponents shall persecute the prophets and apostles who are to be sent by Jesus (Luke 11:50). Some, indeed, shall be killed; and thus the martyrs to come are associated with the martyrs of the past.

Jesus, himself in danger, proceeds to warn his followers. Luke brings to this place his parallels to Matthew's discourse.

Do not fear them who kill the body merely. Your Father knows even of the sparrow's fall, and you are of greater value than sparrows. I say to you that whoever shall confess in me before men the son of man shall confess in him before God's angels, but whoever shall deny me before men shall be denied before God's angels. . . . . When they bring you before the synagogues, the rulers, and the authorities, do not be anxious how or what you shall answer or what you shall say in defense, for the Holy Spirit shall teach you in that moment what you must say [12:4–12].

It is interesting that when Matthew compiles the dramatic discourse against the scribes and Pharisees he, too, causes Jesus to predict persecution. As Luke (11:49) reads, "I shall send to them prophets and apostles; some of them they shall kill and persecute," so Matthew reports, "I send to you prophets, wise men, and scribes; some you shall kill and crucify, and some you shall scourge in your synagogues and persecute from city to city" (23: 24). But, as has been noticed, he does not group with this saying the materials which are so connected in Luke, but distributes them otherwise.

It is obvious, then, that Matthew and Luke have sayings about persecution, some of which ultimately have Mark as their source, others unrelated to Mark. The primitive martyrology is responsible for some, but not all, of the sayings in the later gospels which reflect the martyr interest.

Another well-known saying which must be understood in the light of persecution is the beatitude:

Blessed are they who have been persecuted on account of justness, for theirs is the kingdom of the heavens. Blessed are you when they shall revile you and persecute you, and say everything evil of you falsely on account of me. Rejoice, be glad, for your reward in the heavens is abundant. For it was thus that they persecuted the prophets before you [Matt. 5:10–12].

Luke's parallel to this is less specific, involving less directly persecutory activity. But, like Matthew, it is couched in the familiar language of reward (Luke 6:22 f.). It is worthy of note that use is made in the saying of predictive prophecy and example derived from Scripture. These are sanctions of which much use was made in the later martyrological literature.

Mention must be made of still more additions in Matthew and Luke to Mark's materials which involve the martyr interest. An example is furnished by Luke's report of Herod's purpose to kill Jesus. Jesus' reply is definitely martyrological; it states the purpose of suffering martyrdom at the proper time with a martyr's dignity (Luke 13:31-33). Another instance is the Matthew-Luke parallel saying, differently placed, about the siege of Jerusalem, with Jesus' lament over it (Matt. 23:37-39; Luke 13:34 f.). The special interest of Luke in the destruction of Jerusalem is evident in the alterations of and additions to the "Little Apocalypse" of Mark (Luke 21:20, 24, 25*b*, 26, 28).

The martyr interest is not absent from the latest of the gospels. It is clear that when Mark organized the materials of his story of Jesus' death into the passion story he set a type which became normative for his followers. To be sure, they introduce modifications. But the picture of the martyr Jesus is the essential element in all four relations of the story of the last days. The widest variation occurs in John, where the long discourse on the New Society is substituted for the apocalyptic discourse which is followed, with additions, by Matthew and Luke.

But the Fourth Gospel is the most thoroughgoing of the four in picturing Jesus as the deliberate martyr. True, it finds the mechanisms which cause his death in Jewish opposition, but this is outer and incidental. Jesus' death is the voluntary act by which he draws the world to himself. Therefore Jesus calmly directs the course of events. All others, including the state, are merely contributing

factors. Jesus lays down his life. He dismisses it.
The plan is his Father's, which he carries out. With
gentle dignity he moves from one point to the next.
Pilate explicitly declares his innocence; his death
was voluntary martyrdom.

The Fourth Gospel carries also an interest in the
death of Peter—that is, the Fourth Gospel in the
form which contains the epilogue of chapter 21.
The consciousness of Peter's death was important;
therefore the notable event is explained as in this
source; Peter was one who should be coerced by the
ruthless force resulting in his death. The interest in
notable martyrs is to be found in the Fourth Gospel.

Of teaching directed to this theme there is to be
mentioned the prediction of persecution which appears in Jesus' long discourse on the New Society:
"They shall put you out of the synagogues; indeed,
the hour is coming when whoever kills you shall
think that he is offering service to God." The
teaching, it is said, is given as warning, so that the
followers shall not be caused to stumble (16:1 f.).
Earlier in the same discourse more general statement is made; Jesus has been persecuted, and in
like manner his followers shall be persecuted
(15:20).

These are the reflections of the martyr interest
which the gospels exhibit in their content. How are
they to be understood? They are in part didactic
sayings, in part apocalyptic portents, and in part
editorial and narrative in character. They belong
to the general stream of gospel materials, so that

it is proper to apply social-historical method in the attempt to understand them.

Recent studies of gospel materials have refined this method so that it is readily available. In general it may be said that less significance is attached to the phenomena of literary relation, with correspondingly more attention given the situations in the communities in which the writings were produced. Situation, rather than literary parallelism, is important in the social-historical method.

This is true in a measure of that work upon the gospels which, having risen in Germany, is generally known as *Formgeschichte*. This type of analysis also looks to the communities in and for which the gospels were written. First of all, it subjects the sources to analysis, to discover the "forms" in which the data of the story of Jesus are shaped. The attempt is then made to determine which of these forms are relatively the earlier and which are later; obviously, those clearly recognized as late are identified as unhistorical. The materials of the several forms are studied similarly to isolate the original from the accretions. It is thought that the process of gospel-writing was the putting into shape, on the basis of the various interests which were important to the several local communities, of the materials which had long since taken shape in these various "forms."

Of the two most important scholars who have developed the methods of *Formgeschichte*, Dibelius[1]

[1] Martin Dibelius, *Formgeschichte des Evangeliums* (Tübingen, 1919).

the more intimately relates the gospel materials to the preaching of the followers of Jesus. He very frankly recognizes the meager degree to which the preachers, such as Paul, for example, referred to events of Jesus' life; still less to anything which Jesus taught. Dibelius often implies that it was the need of the Hellenistic community which caused the rise of alleged teachings of Jesus. Bultmann,[1] on the other hand, regards the Palestinian communities as the places where the forms had their rise. He thinks that the accomplishment of the Hellenistic communities was the using of the materials current in the several "forms" in the construction of the gospels. The gospels were the creation of the Hellenistic communities; their materials were, however, produced in the groups of Palestinian disciples. Thus Bultmann appears to believe that these early disciples remembered more or less of that which had indeed come from Jesus. However, he recognizes that much certainly must be ascribed to the communities rather than to Jesus. It is doubtful whether the sayings on persecution go back to Jesus.[2]

It is important to recognize, however individual judgments may disagree, that the basic point of the method of form-history is its reference to the religious communities. It is constantly maintained that the total content of the gospels as wholes or as

[1] Rudolf Bultmann, *Die Geschichte der synoptischen Tradition* (Göttingen, 1921).

[2] Bultmann, *op. cit.*, pp. 67 f., 74, 216.

parts took shape in response to the needs of the Christians as they grouped themselves in societies. It may be affirmed that Dibelius is right in citing the examples of the Pauline groups. It is clear that, so long as Paul's own judgment permitted him to determine what was the proper course for the guidance of his churches, nothing more was needed. When, however, he felt a lack of confidence in his own judgment, Paul appears to have appealed to a "commandment of the Lord" (I Cor. 7:10, 25, 40). It is of indubitable significance that Paul does not quote Jesus. Presumably such "commandments" were derived from ecstatic experience.

But it was exactly in such situations that the need of teachings of Jesus became most clearly felt. A dominating personality was an adequate source, so long as he was available for instruction; but in his absence another authority was necessary. Ecstatic experience characterized many, no doubt, but not all of the churchmen. Furthermore, it is likely that ecstatic revelations disagreed as different persons were inspired. Inevitably a concrete norm, a body of teaching, had to be developed, to take the place of leaders who could not be present everywhere and to dominate in the variety of individualistic inspirations.

This function was fulfilled by the gospels. They appeared as the creative and forceful leaders began to be succeeded by their disciples. The gospel materials supplied the growing congregations with the normative teaching which was vitally necessary to meet the increasing complexities of Christian experience as the horizons of expansion widened.

Social-historical method[1] believes frankly that the needs of the Christian communities acted as the producing causes for the rise of the moral codes represented by the gospel teachings. It is recognized that between the earliest gospel and the days of Jesus there is a gap which cannot be bridged by mere literary analysis. It is not expected that the primitive sources of the gospels may be discovered by literary methods. Such hypothetical documents as have been reconstructed are found to be only some few steps nearer Jesus than the gospels themselves. Consequently such sources are to be interrogated as the gospels are interrogated, and answers may be obtained only in the same manner and degree as they are gained from the study of the gospels.

Social-historical method thus identifies the teachings of Jesus in the gospels (or their sources) by reference to the Palestinian-Jewish environment of Jesus on the one hand, and to the Hellenistic communities on the other. Agreement with known environment is the criterion by which a datum is identified as authentic, that is, having actually come from Jesus or as having been produced by a Christian community. In such cases as suggest agreement with Graeco-Roman situations, it is concluded that the teaching, even though ascribed in a

[1] S. J. Case, *Jesus, A New Biography* (Chicago, 1928), pp. 57–115, especially pp. 103–15.

gospel to Jesus, was actually produced later by a Christian group. It is thought that these were ascribed to Jesus to gain authority for them. The alleged teachings of Jesus were used as normative standards, and of course the ascription of them to Jesus operated as a powerful sanction.

An immediate effect of the application of historical method of any school to the gospels is the discrimination of a certain amount of unhistorical accretion from the resultant historical original. Such has been accomplished by no small number of studies of the life and teaching of Jesus. Exactly what remains in the judgment of the researcher as the final historical residuum is not always in agreement with the findings of others. Obviously the result depends to a degree upon the method followed.

It is equally obvious that much in the result of the application of a method depends upon the particular matters to which research is directed. It is indisputable, for example, that the roots of gospel apocalyptic go down into Palestinian Judaism. On the other hand, it is probable that the story of Jesus' conception and birth as told in the Gospel according to Luke came from, since it correlates with the familiar myths of, Hellenistic religion. Clearly, some of the gospel materials reflect the secondary situations more apparently than others.

Certainly, of all the gospel traditions the sayings about persecution lend themselves with unsurpassed readiness to social-historical interpretation. The application of the method is not difficult in their case. These questions are asked: To what experiences of Jesus do these sayings relate themselves? To what relative degree do these sayings correlate with the known environment of Jesus? Finally, to what relative degree do they correlate with the known environment and experiences of Jesus' followers, the Christians of the Graeco-Roman world?

Clearly, the gospel sayings about persecution do not purport to have been uttered with reference to Jesus' experiences. Much as the Gospels picture the suffering Jesus; much as they subtly suggest Jesus the martyr, they do not report the persecution logia with reference to his own fate. These sayings are concerned rather with the fate of his followers.

May they, however, be considered as genuine predictions? Were the experiences of Jesus harsh enough to warn him that such also were to be expected by his followers?

It must be recognized that research has markedly changed the usual point of view which found in the dialectical conflicts of Jesus and his Jewish opponents the basis for the sayings about persecution. It is now known that, so far as the intellectual side of Judaism was concerned, a wide freedom was allowed. It is extremely unlikely that doctrinal difference with other teachers had anything to do with Jesus' death. It has long been known that, while the Pharisees might dispute, they would not persecute. The death of Jesus, so far as Jewish leaders were involved, was occasioned by those professionally interested in maintaining the *status quo*. The immediate means was the Roman court, and presumably the occasion was a political implication.

Thus the sayings about persecution, considered as Jesus' words, have an academic ring. They lack the essential relevance to relate them to actual experience, or the aspect of immediate practicability to enable them to be regarded as genuine predictions.

When, however, the persecution logia are regarded in the light of the known experiences of the early Christians, they are relevant. They do relate themselves to actual situations. They appear to have been eminently practical. Certainly there were many occasions which were such as to make these sayings usable. It is altogether proper to examine them in the light of such situations.

The traditional persecution situations are, of course, the first to suggest themselves. The traditions of Acts have several. The Jewish leaders forcibly opposed the early Christian leaders, Acts reports. The death of Stephen is a well-known example. Herod Agrippa I, in the interim between procurators, is said to have caused the martyr death of James (the son of Zebedee). The persecuting activity of Paul is emphasized. Persecution is alleged as the immediate cause of the scattering of the Jerusalem disciples, and thus as the innocent reason for the carrying of the new movement to Antioch. Paul, after his change of faith, is described as suffering persecution on several occasions, finally becoming so involved that several reviews of his case are reported, with Acts closing as Paul remains a prisoner in Rome.

The letters of Paul, too, contain references to persecution. There is the long list of Paul's own sufferings, some of which are of this nature, in II Corinthians (11:23–33). An early letter, I Thessalonians, speaks of ill treatment at Phillippi (2:2), and refers also to suffering on the part of the churches (2:14). In the letter to the Galatians Paul refers to his own former activity as a persecutor (1:13, 23), and implies definitely that he was now being persecuted (5:11). Moreover, the same letter avows that opponents were guilty of persecuting anyone who preached an unwelcome teaching (6:12).

Paul's difficulties with the state are obviously reflected in his letters. Philippians is perhaps the readiest example (1:17, 21, 28–30; 3:6, 10; 4:14). A recent commentary on Philippians[1] is an interesting example of the manner by which persecution is used as a clue for the understanding of the letter itself, and is recognized as a force which operated to crystallize the thought of the early Christians.

It is plain that these references and traditions are themselves in need of study. Some of them point to Jewish opposition, while others involve the state as the coercive force. Now, a thorough examination of the alleged Jewish persecutions has been made by Abrahams.[2] He concludes that Jewish op-

[1] Ernst Lohmeyer, *Der Brief an die Philipper* (Göttingen, 1928).

[2] Abrahams, *Studies in Pharisaism and the Gospels* (2d Ser., Cambridge, 1924), pp. 67–69.

position was purely doctrinal, and was urged didactically. It is denied that opposition reached the place of persecution, except perhaps an uncontrollable mob action occurred. Such traditions as that of *The Martyrdom of Polycarp* (xiii. 1), that the Jews were zealous in encompassing the death of Christinas, are regarded as unhistorical.

Recent study of the Book of Acts does not warrant the placing of confidence in its traditions of persecution.[1] The literature of which Acts is a part belongs to the rise of apologetic, and had as an important purpose the proof of Christianity's political innocence. These traditions actually point to the state as the source of danger to the early Christians.

It is therefore urged that the background which has been furnished by the present study offers the sufficient clue for the understanding of the sayings on persecution. It is urged, in short, that the relation of Christians to the state produced the entire literature on martyrdom, including the gospel sayings on persecution. These sayings are properly interpreted by the social-historical method, which, it is hoped, is shown by the present study to be adequate (indeed, to be the only adequate method) to make them fully intelligible. No doubt, emerging Christianity, as is true of every new religion, had to face opposition. No doubt, some of this opposition was physical. It is altogether likely, whatever may have been the case later, that other leaders beside Paul were beaten in synagogues. The prob-

[1] Riddle, *op. cit.*, pp. 56–66, 149 ff.

ability is great that the sayings which put into Jesus' mouth predictions of persecution by Jews were produced as the Christians suffered such experiences and derived comfort from the developing traditions of teachings of Jesus.

But some, perhaps the most, of the alleged sayings of Jesus about persecution demand activity on the part of the state to make their production intelligible. Perhaps the traditional opposition of Herod Agrippa I, resulting in the martyrdom of James and wider persecution of others, accounts for some of the sayings.[1] The sayings about confession and denial, technical as they are, necessitate state punishment for their understanding. These terms, referring to court testimony, can hardly be taken in the Pauline sense of the confession or denial of Jesus as Lord. The use with them of the sanctions of reward and punishment aligns them with the later use by the church leaders in definitely known situations of persecution.

To answer the crucial question, whether previous to the composition of the Gospels there were situations to produce these sayings, requires inference. But, since in Roman law every new cult or society was illegal, it is inherently probable that upon many an occasion of which nothing is known the law may have been applied. The Book of Acts, of course, is anxious to show that in all such cases as that thrown out of court by Gallio, the new cult

[1] Cf. Bacon, "Pharisees and Herodians in Mark," *Journal of Biblical Literature*, XXXIX (1911), 102–12.

was not suppressed. But such a tradition as this may be regarded as highly tendencious. There is no doubt that some of the sufferings mentioned by Paul were occasioned by his becoming involved with the Roman law. One may, with entire confidence, infer that similar cases were common in the experiences of other leaders.

At all events, a survey of the attitudes of the Christians to persecution, seen in their entire range of development, suggests that, as methods of control were produced in later situations, methods were doubtless developed in earlier situations. It may be concluded that the gospel sayings about persecution were produced by the early Christian communities, or by the leaders who articulated the attitudes current in the communities. The sayings were put in the form of words of Jesus because this, above all other forms, secured sanction for them.

It is to be concluded that the martyr interest was effective in the content of the gospels as well as in their literary type. They picture Jesus as a martyr, and cryptically refer to the martyrdom of other heroes, and thus function as practical martyrologies. But they have as a purpose, together with other objects, the securing of proper attitudes on the part of their publics. To be sure, they recommend a dependence upon charismatic inspiration to secure a confession—a method which subsequent experience found to be impracticable and in consequence discarded. But the gospels devote themselves, as do other and later types of literature, to the task of securing confessions. They aim to assist in the maintenance of the integrity of the religious groups, even though this involved martyrdom for some of their adherents. The necessity of securing control in persecution became apparent in Christian leadership as early as the production of the gospel materials, and in this necessity the martyr interest was a notable producing factor.

Persecution was therefore a major influence upon early Christianity. As it is viewed in situations where the sources permit an intimate acquaintance with Christian life, the entire technique of control is discoverable. It is possible to work from the periods in which information is abundant, admitting confident generalization, toward the earlier periods in which the sources are less adequate. If one safeguards his generalizations, it is still possible to observe the Christian groups in situations which are similar in nature to those well known. That one may, in view of the assured findings in the maturer periods, progress from these to the very formative periods of the Christian movement is especially fortunate. It is most gratifying that, as attention is being directed to the study of religion for social control, the data of the persecution of the Christians furnish so accessible a field of investigation. The leadership of Christianity's early days was able to develop techniques of social control. As today's problems bring their needs, it is altogether probable that much may be learned from the study of the behavior of the martyrs.

INDEX

INDEX

I. PERSONS AND SUBJECTS

II. SOURCES

DATE DUE

GAYLORD			PRINTED IN U.S.A.